Music Express Xtra

Listening to Music History

Active listening materials to support a school music scheme

Compiled and written by
Helen MacGregor

Illustrated by
Alison Dexter

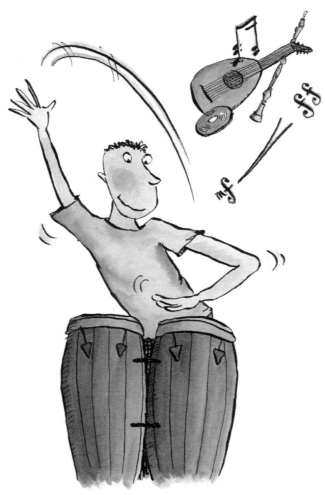

A&C Black • London
Produced in association with *hyperion*

Introduction

The Listening to Music series offers an imaginative approach to understanding and making music in the classroom. Through practical activities and active listening, children develop an understanding of other people's music, which they can then apply to their own performances and compositions.

This *History* pack provides an introduction to an inspiring range of western music from the medieval devotional songs of Hildegard of Bingen to the exciting late 20th century dance music of Eleanor Alberga.

HOW THE PACK IS ORGANISED

Six separate sections cover the major periods of western musical history: medieval, renaissance, baroque, classical, romantic and 20th century. These are commonly-used categories, which are useful for identifying styles and developments.

Each section presents:

- three complete pieces of music with closely related class, group and individual activities for whiteboard display, download or photocopying;

- three 'listening link' extracts with worksheet activities to help further assess the children's individual knowledge and understanding of the music.

Some of the listening links complement one of the three complete pieces; the others are supplementary – broadening the experience of music from a particular period. (All should be preceded by the activities on the three complete works.)

This new edition of *Listening to Music History* comprises a book of teaching notes and two enhanced CDs, which contain all of the necessary audio recordings, together with supporting materials for whiteboard display. (Please note that permission to photocopy extends only to the whiteboard pdfs, and that photocopies may only be used for the teaching purposes specified in this book.) The enhanced CDs are for use in a conventional CD player (audio CD tracks) or to access the whiteboard materials on computer: load the CD into your computer and click on the start icon that will appear on your desktop.

Within each whiteboard section, an introductory page allows you to navigate directly to an activity. Alternatively, you can navigate between displays using the back and forward buttons in the top right-hand corner of each. Where appropriate, audio is embedded into the whiteboard display. Click on the CD icon to listen to the recording. CD icons without a track number link to additional supplementary tracks that do not feature on the audio CD. For all but the shortest tracks, a control panel will appear when you click on the CD icon. Also included on the enhanced CD are six sample lesson plans, a sample of how to integrate Listening to Music History activities into a school music scheme and staff notation of 15 songs and instrumental parts from the activities for music readers.

The selection of music

The music selected gives a sample of sounds from each period and an indication of how music has changed over the centuries. It does not aim to give a complete picture.

Change in music comes about through a mix of development from within, and an influence from outside – change in society for instance. What does not change, however, are the elements of music. Duration, dynamics, tempo, timbre, pitch and structure are as fundamental to medieval music as they are to the music of the present day. All the activities are firmly rooted in these elements and will help children to recognise a common ground between their own music and that of the past.

Each piece of music has been chosen for its appeal and accessibility to children, and because it lends itself to activities which offer a wide range of skill development.

Social context is explored throughout and some choices will be particularly relevant to work in the history curriculum. For instance, during the renaissance, we have focussed on Tudor music, while in the 20th century section you will find Copland's fanfare for the Allied troops of World War II.

Tuned percussion notation

Tuned percussion notes are given as letter names and it is necessary to show the difference between high notes and low notes of the same letter name. A small dash indicates this, eg

C, is lower than C which is in turn lower than C'

hyperion

Finally, we wish to acknowledge our gratitude to Hyperion, whose complete support and generous access to the wealth of recordings in their catalogue have made this pack possible. To find out more about the CDs from which this selection is drawn, turn to page 4.

Second edition 2009
A&C Black Ltd
36 Soho Square, London W1D 3QY
© 2009, 1998 A&C Black Ltd
ISBN 978-0-7136-8399-8

Text © 2009, 1998 Helen MacGregor
Illustrations © 2009, 1998 Alison Dexter
Sound recording © 2009, 1998 A&C Black
Cover illustration © 2009 Moira Munro
CD-ROM © 2009 A&C Black

Edited and developed by Sheena Roberts and Lucy Mitchell
Designed by Fiona Grant
Sound engineered by Stephen Chadwick

CD-ROM post-production by Ian Shepherd at Sound Recording Technology
Music setting by Jenny Roberts
Printed in Great Britain by Caligraving Ltd, Thetford, Norfolk

Contents

 1))) **Audio tracks** (track lists on inside back cover).

- All the recordings you need for each activity.

These recordings include the title recordings for each section plus numerous support recordings which give extra help with understanding activities. Clear references to the track numbers required are given next to each activity and within the text.

 WB 1 **Whiteboard displays** with embedded audio.

- Display/printouts with embedded audio for whiteboard display or printout.

These offer an alternative route through the content of the book and its associated recordings. Every activity is represented in one or more display pdfs with embedded audio. The activities are ordered exactly as they appear in the book and contain concise instructions directed to the children. These instructions may be supplemented by referring to the book itself as required.

Acknowledgements

The copyright recordings listed below have been used by permission of

hyperion

PO Box 25, London SE9 1AX, Tel 020 8318 1234
email info@hyperion-records.co.uk
website www.hyperion-records.co.uk:

Columba aspexit (English translation by Christopher Page) and **O viridissima virga** by Abbess Hildegard of Bingen (1098–1179) from *A feather on a the breath of God*, performed by *Gothic Voices* with Emma Kirkby. Catalogue number **CDA66039**.

Estampie Royal (no 4), **Danse Royale** (no 2), by anonymous composers; **Eno sagrado en Vigo** and **Aj ondas que eu vin veer** by Martin Codax (fl.1230) (both English translations by Stephen Haynes) from *Bella Domna*, performed by *Sinfonye* with Maria Kiek (voice), directed by Stevie Wishart. Cat number **CDH55207**.

Mistress Winter's Jump and **Suzanna** by John Dowland (1563–1626) from *Consort Music by John Dowland*, performed by *Extempore String Ensemble* directed by George Weigand. Cat number **A66010**.

Pueri, concinite by Jacob Handl (1550–1591) from *Christmas Music from Medieval and Renaissance Europe*, performed by *The Sixteen* directed by Harry Christophers. Cat number **CDA66263**.

Martin said to his man by Thomas Ravenscroft (c1582–c1635) and **Packington's Pound** by an Anonymous composer from *How the world wags*, performed by *The City Waites*. Cat number **CDH55013**.

In nomine II by Richard Atwood (fl.1550) from *For His Majesty's Sagbutts and Cornetts* performed by *His Majesty's Sagbutts and Cornetts*. Cat number **CDA66894**.

Chiacona by Tarquinio Merula (1594–1665) and **Canzona super entrada aechiopicam** (Canzona super cantionem gallicam 'Est-ce mars?') by Samuel Scheidt (1587–1654) from *His Majesty's Sagbutts and Cornetts Grand Tour*, performed by *His Majesty's Sagbutts and Cornetts*. Cat number **CDA66847**.

Recorder Concerto in A minor (Concerto in A minor, RV108) by Antonio Vivaldi (1678–1741) from *Vivaldi Recorder Concertos*, performed by Peter Holtslag and *The Parley of Instruments*. Cat number **CDH55016**.

Chorus Lebe, Sonne dieser Erden from The 'Hunt' Cantata (Cantata 208) by Johann Sebastian Bach (1685–1750) from *Wedding Cantata & Bach Hunt Cantata*, performed by *The Parley of Instruments* directed by Roy Goodman. Cat number **CDD22041**.

The 'Hen' Symphony (Symphony no 83 in G minor) by Franz Joseph Haydn (1732–1809) from *Symphonies of Haydn*, performed by *The Hanover Band* directed by Roy Goodman. Cat number **CDH55123**.

A Christmas Carol (Let an anthem of praise) Anonymous Baroque, arr. Caleb Ashworth (1722–1775) from *While Shepherds Watched* performed by *Psalmody* and *The Parley of Instruments* directed by Peter Holman. Cat number **CDH55325**.

Variations in F major on 'Ein Mädchen oder Weibchen' from Mozart's Die Zauberflöte, Op 66 by Ludwig van Beethoven (1770–1827) from *Beethoven's Complete Cello Music – Sonatas* performed by Melvyn Tan (fortepiano), Anthony Pleeth (cello). Cat number **CDD22004**.

The 'Trout' Quintet (Piano Quintet in A Major, D667) by Franz Peter Schubert (1797–1828) from *Hummel, Schubert & Schumann*, performed by *The Schubert Ensemble of London*. Cat number **CDD22008**.

Polka by Alexander Borodin (1833–1887) and **Le Rossignol** by Franz Liszt (1811–1886) from *Liszt: The complete music for solo piano, Vol. 35 – Arabesques* performed by Leslie Howard & Philip Moore. Cat number **CDA66984**.

Sursum corda by Sir Edward Elgar (1857–1934), **Paris Fanfare** by Paul Patterson (b1947), and **Konzertmusik** (op 50) by Paul Hindemith (1895–1963) from *The Royal Eurostar and other brass music*, performed by *London Brass Virtuosi*, *The Philharmonia Orchestra* and Joseph Cullen (organ), directed by David Honeyball. Cat number **CDA66870**.

Fanfare for the common man by Aaron Copland (1900–1990) from *Music for Brass and Percussion*, performed by *London Brass Virtuosi* directed by David Honeyball. Cat number **CDA66189**.

Gnossienne no 3 arranged for orchestra by Ronald Corp, and **La nuit** (from **Mercure**) by Erik Satie (1866–1925) from *Satie's Theatre Music* performed by *New London Orchestra* directed by Ronald Corp. Cat number **CDH55176**.

Translations of **Columba aspexit**, **Eno sagrado en Vigo** and **Aj ondas que eu vin veer** © Hyperion.

Details of all recordings, including lyrics, clips and composer information, are available at www.hyperion-records.co.uk

The following copyrights recordings and content have been included by kind permission of the copyright holders:

Sextet from Dancing with the Shadow by Eleanor Alberga from *British Women Composers – Vol 2* released by Lontano Records Ltd, 35 A Copeland Road, London E17 9DB. Cat number **LNT103**.

Ein Mädchen oder Weibchen from Die Zauberflöte performed by *Drottingholm Concert Theatre* directed by Östman © PolyGram. Cat number Decca Classics **440 085–2**.

Waltz from Serenade for Strings performed by *Netherlands Symphony Orchestra* directed by Zinman © PolyGram. Cat number Philips Classics **438 748–2**.

Graphic score of **Fanfare for the common man** by Aaron Copland. Copyright 1944 by the Aaron Copland Fund for Music, Inc. Copyright renewed. Boosey & Hawkes, Inc. Sole licensee. Reproduced by permission of Boosey & Hawkes Music Publishers Ltd.

O maiden come to join me (translation by Andrew Porter of the first verse of Ein Mädchen oder Weibchen) © Faber Music Ltd.

All other recordings produced by A&C Black:

Sonata for harpsichord, performed by Timothy Roberts; **The candle** (by Alasdair MacGregor) and melody of **Martin said to his man** performed by Rosamund Chadwick; Melody of **A Christmas carol**, melody of **O maiden come to join me** and **The hen chant** performed by Vivien Ellis ; **Chiacona** ground bass and decorations performed by Timothy Roberts (harpsichord) and Jeremy West (cornett). Voice overs by Jonathan Trueman, Helen MacGregor, Stephen Chadwick and Sheena Roberts. All other supplementary recordings devised and performed by Helen MacGregor and Stephen Chadwick © A&C Black.

Medieval introduction

WHAT YOU NEED TO KNOW ABOUT THE MEDIEVAL PERIOD

★ When Christianity spread across Europe after the fall of the Roman Empire in 410 AD, monasteries became centres for composing and performing music. Religious services often included dancing, singing and playing instruments.

★ A tradition of singing simple, flowing melodies, called plainchant, became part of the celebration of mass. The tradition survives to this day.

★ Plainchant, or plainsong, was originally passed on orally, varying in style from region to region or monastery to monastery. Then, to preserve traditions, religious communities began devising methods of writing down the music.

★ At first, signs were added to the text to give some indication of the rhythms. Later, the signs were placed at different levels above the words to show where the melodies moved up or down in pitch.

★ In the 10th century, Guido d'Arezzo (d 1050), an Italian monk and teacher, set down the idea of placing notes on or between a set of parallel lines – the stave – thus fixing their pitch in relation to each other.

★ Staff notation (writing music on a stave) is now established as the internationally recognised language of music, although, throughout history, many alternative systems have been developed and are used in different parts of the world.

★ During this time, professional travelling musicians – minstrels – entertained people. From the 11th to the 13th centuries, groups of jugglers, dancers, acrobats and minstrels provided popular entertainment in town and countryside.

★ Popular dances and melodies were spread by the minstrels from country to country, and although many were not written down until later times, they survived in the folk dances and songs of the people.

★ At the same time, male and female poet-musicians, based in royal courts, and often themselves courtiers of noble birth, were composing sophisticated songs for the entertainment of the nobility of Europe. They sang of chivalry, love, nature, and tales of the Crusades.

★ The poet-musician was called a troubadour in Southern Europe and a trouvère in France.

★ Music of this time was based on different sets of notes from those most commonly used later. These sets of notes were known as modes. You can hear what they sound like by playing any set of eight adjacent white keys on a keyboard, eg D E F G A B C D. The modes survive in some folk and jazz music.

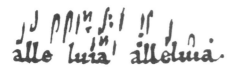

Two early forms of music notation

Medieval Columba aspexit

WHAT YOU NEED TO KNOW ABOUT COLUMBA ASPEXIT
Composer: Hildegard of Bingen (1098–1179)

★ Hildegard was educated from the age of eight at a Benedictine nunnery. She became Abbess of the nunnery when she was 38 and later moved to the convent of Bingen (in modern Germany).

★ She wrote extensively on theology, natural history, medicine and the many visions she had seen since childhood. Through extensive letter-writing she was involved in diplomacy and politics, spreading her fame across Europe.

★ Hildegard was also a musician who composed many large-scale devotional songs, of which **Columba aspexit** is an example. The Latin text presents a vivid picture of Saint Maximinus celebrating mass, and was probably written for the abbey of which he was patron.

Features of the music

★ The melody does not have a steady beat, but flows freely, following the rhythm of the words.

★ The melody moves mostly step-by-step to higher or lower notes, with few jumps in pitch.

★ There are many examples of melisma – one syllable of the text stretched over two or more notes of the melody, eg *bal-sa——mum...*

★ One singer leads with the first line of text, then alternates with a group of voices singing together.

Drone accompaniment

★ The singers are accompanied by a symphony (see below) playing a drone. A drone – the repetition of a single note or combination of notes throughout a piece of music – was a common accompaniment to music of this time.

Symphony – hurdy gurdy

★ The symphony, or hurdy gurdy, was a popular instrument during the 12th century, used for both religious and secular music. It was the first instrument to combine strings with a keyboard.

★ The player turns a wheel which vibrates drone strings. As well as this drone, a melody can be played on a keyboard which operates a separate string or strings. Hurdy gurdies are still used today in French and Belgian folk music.

ABOUT THE ACTIVITIES

Listen to *Columba aspexit* – focussing on the age of the music and the means of recording it in an age before the invention of sound recording.

Exploring notation – finding a way to notate a simple melody using three next-door notes.

Using notation – in pairs, the children notate their melodies using a horizontal line to indicate the relationship of one note to another and to show the shape of the melody.

Listen to *The candle* – listening to and following the notation of *The candle*, noticing what the notation conveys.

Perform *The candle* – in small groups, the children work out a performance of *The candle*, using the notation.

Listen to Columba aspexit

After listening, tell the children that this music was composed nearly one thousand years ago, long before sound recording was invented.

What you will need

Questions you might ask

- How could the music have been passed on from generation to generation? (It was written down.)
- Explain that musicians in monasteries were only just beginning to find ways of writing down music. How is music written down nowadays? (In staff notation.)

Exploring notation

What you will need

- A set of chime bars (or other tuned percussion) with three next-door notes – DEF (or any others available, eg EFG) for each child.

1. Listen to track 2 (WB2). How might this sequence of notes be written down? Discuss the children's ideas for doing this. Here are three examples of the sequence written in different ways:

D E F D F E D

2. Discuss problems with these notations, eg letter names alone don't help the reader to see the shape of the melody; a line showing a shape doesn't say which notes to use.

3. Next, the children individually prepare a short piece of descriptive prose (eg see **The candle**) about themselves or related to a class topic (WB3).

4. The children (each using a set of chime bars with notes D E F) compose a melody for their words, notating it in their chosen way.

5. Listen to the melodies together, discussing the different notations the children have devised, eg how well they work, what problems arose. (Letter names alone don't help the reader to see the shape of the melody. A line showing the shape doesn't say which note to sing, etc.)

Using line notation

1. Remind the children of the problems they may have found in their exploration of notation.

2. Explain that early musicians settled on the idea of using a horizontal line to show the relationship of higher to lower notes (this eventually led to modern staff notation):

3. Each child now rewrites their composition (page 7) on line notation, using either letter names or symbols as above.

4. With their partner, they sing and play each melody in turn, reading from their notation.

   Does the performance highlight more problems? Are there other things than pitch to show? (Some notes may last longer than others; more than one note may be sung to one syllable.)

   What additions or revisions might be made to assist an accurate performance?

What you will need

 WB 4

• Tuned percussion for pairs of children and writing materials.

Teaching tip

Assess whether the children have understood how notation needs to indicate pitch clearly, and that pitch alone is not enough – rhythm needs to be shown as well. (Notation went on developing until this was achieved.)

Listen to The candle

As you listen, follow the notation of the music together (opposite and on WB5).

What you will need

 3))) WB 5

Questions you might ask

• How has the composer notated the music? (Using dots positioned on two lines.)

• How many different notes has the composer used? (Five different pitches.)

• Which is the highest-sounding note? (The one which rests in the space above the upper line.) Which is the lowest-sounding note? Etc.

• What do the curved lines above some of the notes show? (These lines show when a word/syllable is sung to more than one note.)

• What else does the music show? (The little pictures of instruments show extra sounds.)

• What doesn't the music show? (It doesn't show the rhythm very clearly; it doesn't show what the other instruments play.)

• What else can you hear in the music? (There is a long ringing sound all the time in the background; someone is playing a drone.)

What you will need

- Tuned percussion for each small group of children:

– a tuned instrument with notes:

– a drone instrument with notes:

– a drum, maraca, tambourine and cymbal with soft beater.

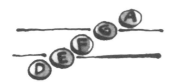

Key to letter names of notes

Teaching tips

Learning the melody of *The candle*: the children might take it in turns to play each line on tuned percussion, singing it back immediately. Practise like this until all can sing the whole song together.

Adding a drone: if using tuned percussion, the players will need to use two beaters, alternating them quickly to achieve a long ringing sound.

Perform The candle

1. Each group has a copy of *The candle* and works out the melody on tuned percussion, using the key to the letter names of the notes.

2. Learn each line of the melody separately until you can all sing the whole song.

3. Add a drone using notes D and A – or just D.

4. The children decide what sounds to add on each line using a drum, then maraca, then tambourine, then cymbal. They work out a way of writing down what they are playing, using the space below the words.

It looks like a vol-ca-no, blue, white and purple

The wax is the la-va, craw——ling down the side

The flame is the la-va, ro-cket-ing in-to the sky

And the light is as bright as a mil-lion stars and the sun

Medieval Estampie royal

WHAT YOU NEED TO KNOW ABOUT ESTAMPIE ROYAL
Composer: anonymous (13th century)

Dance music and the estampie

✦ Estampies are dances played on instruments. They were the first dances for pairs of men and women, each couple dancing together holding hands. Before the estampie, dances were performed with songs, everyone joining in with the dancing in a line or a circle.

✦ Estampies were possibly the earliest form of purely instrumental music. They originated in Provence, then were spread through Europe by troubadours escaping the Albigensian Crusades at the beginning of the 13th century.

✦ Though the estampie was a very popular dance throughout Europe until the 14th century – often danced in the open air – only a few of its steps are known today.

The instruments

✦ Many court musicians, who had travelled with the crusaders during the holy wars against the Muslims, heard the instruments and music of North Africa and the Middle East, which influenced their own compositions.

✦ This estampie is played on a traditional Moroccan hand-played frame drum with rattles (below right) and on medieval fiddle (below left). The illustrations are drawn from contemporary images.

Features of the music

✦ A rousing rhythm is played on frame drum.

✦ The melody is played on the medieval fiddle.

✦ After a short drum introduction, the fiddle enters. There are two main sections, A and B, within which improvised (made up) melodies are alternated with a refrain (recurring melody). The piece ends with the drum played on its own again.

ABOUT THE ACTIVITIES

Listen to *Estampie royal* – the class focus on the structure of the piece, noticing the pattern of counts into which the sections fall.

Percussion estampie – small groups rehearse and present a percussion performance based on the structure of *Estampie royal*.

What you will need

 4-5))) WB 6-7

• Enlarged printout of the chart or WB6-7.

Listen to Estampie royal

1. As a class, practise counting along with the music of *Estampie royal*, track 4 (WB6).

2. Listen to *Estampie royal*, track 5 (WB7). Ask a volunteer to point to the numbers on the chart (WB7), as the others count them out loud.

Questions you might ask

• What pattern do the numbers make in the A sections? (4 – 7 – 4 – 8)

• What is the number pattern in the B sections? (6 – 7 – 6 – 8)

3. This time when you count along as a class, everyone claps hands quietly during the 4- and 6-count sections and taps knees during the 7- and 8-count sections.

4. Repeat. Encourage the children to count silently after the introduction, while maintaining a steady but quiet clap/tap.

Questions you might ask

• What do the children notice about the melody when they are tapping their knees? (The melody of the 7- and 8-count sections is the same – it starts on a low note, then jumps up.)

• What do they notice about the melody when they are clapping? (In the 4- and 6-count sections, the fiddle plays different music each time. It usually starts on higher notes.)

What you will need

 WB 7-8

• Two sets of percussion for each group: all different/all the same eg – wood block, jingles, tambour; – drums.

• A copy of the chart for each group.

Teaching tips

Assess the children's understanding of the number pattern through the questions and practical work.

Ensure that everyone is familiar with the idea of improvising and give individuals turns to demonstrate making up rhythms during the 4- and 6-count sections.

Percussion estampie

1. In groups of six or seven, rehearse and present a percussion performance of *Estampie royal*. Each group appoints a conductor; the others play either all different instruments or all the same.

2. The conductor counts the number patterns; the others tap the beat, eg

   4- and 6-count sections – wood block, jingles and tambour play the beat;
   7- and 8-count sections – drums play the beat.

   What might be improved? Were there any difficulties?

3. When everyone is secure with this, those playing the 7- and 8-count sections devise a rhythm to play instead of tapping the beat. Now the groups perform again (still with the conductor counting):

   4- and 6-count sections – play the beat;
   7- and 8-count sections – drums play their new rhythm.

4. When this is confident, try this:

   4- and 6-count sections – individuals take turns to improvise new rhythms while the others play the beat;
   7- and 8-count sections – drums play their repeated rhythm.

Medieval Cantigas de amigo 1 and 2

WHAT YOU NEED TO KNOW ABOUT CANTIGAS DE AMIGO

Composer: Martin Codax (c1300)

★ Martin Codax was a highly successful troubadour in northern Spain in the latter part of the 13th century.

★ These two contrasting songs – *Eno sagrado en Vigo* and *Aj ondas que eu vin veer* – are from a set of seven poems and music, *Cantigas de amigo*, which were discovered in 1914 on a piece of parchment inside a book binding. They are in the voice of a woman from Vigo, who pines for her lover (amigo/amado) far away. The language is a local Spanish dialect.

Features of *Eno sagrado en Vigo*

★ The song has five short verses, each ending with a one line repeated refrain, 'amor ei'.

★ The melody moves mostly step by step and uses a modal (see page 5) set of notes.

★ A woman sings, accompanied by harp, symphony and a hand-played frame drum in this arrangement.

★ The rhythms have a strong dance-like beat.

★ At the end, the instruments drop out one by one, thinning the texture until only the drone (see page 6) is left. This leads into the next song.

Features of *Aj ondas que eu vin veer*

★ There are two short verses with very similar endings.

★ The melody is slow and wistful, moving step by step and using a modal set of notes.

★ A quiet drone on symphony drops out on the last line.

★ The rhythm freely follows the words with much use of melisma – one syllable stretched across several notes.

ABOUT THE ACTIVITIES

Listen to *Cantigas de amigo 1* and *2* – the class focus on the contrasting mood of the two songs.

Composing to create a mood – working in small groups, the children set a medieval poem to a melody. The aim is to create a distinctive mood reflecting that of the words.

What you will need

6))) WB 9

Listen to Cantigas de amigo 1 and 2

1. Compare the two pieces. As they listen, the children may like to move their hands and bodies.

> **Questions you might ask**
>
> • How did the songs make you feel?
>
> • Did you notice any difference between the two songs and the way you moved?

2. Listen again. What changes the mood? (Notice the tempo of the songs, the way the instruments accompany, the volume of the singing and playing.)

3. Together, look at the translations of the texts (WB9) and compare these with the children's thoughts about the music. The first describes dancing in joy at being in love, the second calls to the sea in sadness at being separated from a loved one. Do the children agree that the music reflects the mood of the texts?

Composing to create a mood

What you will need

WB 10-11

• Copies of either one of the two poems for each group.

• A range of instruments, tuned and untuned.

• Recording equipment.

1. Two poems (WB10-11) give an opportunity for the children, working in small groups, to make up their own melodies to suit the mood of the words.

2. Explain that the groups need to read the poem they have chosen out loud several times. They need to discuss the words and mood and then begin composing their melody to suit. They will need to think about the rhythm and the speed.

3. If possible, let them make a sound recording of their melody so that they can listen to and revise it as necessary to match the words better.

4. When they are satisfied with their melody, they need to choose some instruments to play an accompaniment. Try out the ideas together. Does the accompaniment match the mood?

5. When each group is ready, perform the songs to the class.

6. They may like to notate their melody and illustrate it as a medieval manuscript with pictures and colours.

Teaching tips
Assess how well the children's melodies express the mood of the words. Consider the use of tempo, rhythm, pitch and dynamics – have these been considered and used effectively?
Have any of the groups used a drone, or melisma?

Medieval links

WHAT YOU NEED TO KNOW ABOUT THE MUSIC

The three pieces of music in this section are linked to the three pieces the children have worked on in depth in previous activities. They are further examples of

- devotional music by Hildegard of Bingen;

- courtly dance music;

- music of the troubadours.

O viridissima virga
Composer: Hildegard of Bingen (1098–1179)

The Latin text of this devotional song illustrates Hildegard's devotion to the Virgin Mary. The melody is sung first by a group of tenors (high male voices), then by a single tenor. The drone accompaniment (page 6) is played on the symphony (page 6).

Danse royale
Composer: anon French (c13th century)

A harp plays this court dance. The elegant, slow melody is for the type of graceful, walking dance which the lords and ladies would perform at banquets.

Onques n'amai tant que jou fui amee
Composer: Richart de Fournival (born in Amiens, c1201–60)

This lament –

> 'I never loved as much as I was loved, now I repent
> – through my pride I have lost my love.'

is a 'chanson de femmes', intended to be performed by female court musicians. Its composer was a French poet-musician – a trouvère. Twenty of his poems and six of his songs survive.

The song is accompanied by a medieval fiddle.

ABOUT THE ACTIVITIES

This section enables the children to work independently with three pieces of music which have links to things they have heard and learned during the earlier activities.

What you will need
7))) WB 12

What you will need
8))) WB 13

What you will need
9))) WB 14

ASSESSMENT GUIDANCE

★ Can pupils follow a score which uses fixed line notation as they listen to a simple melody?

★ Can they compose a simple melody with a number of pitches, using fixed line notation?

★ Can they perform and compose a rhythmic piece in a variety of irregular metres?

★ Can they describe how music is used to communicate different moods and effects using a wide range of musical vocabulary?

★ Do they understand how time and place can influence the way music is created, performed and heard?

★ Can they compose music which communicates different moods and effects?

★ Can they suggest improvements to their own and others' work?

Renaissance introduction

WHAT YOU NEED TO KNOW ABOUT THE RENAISSANCE

★ This was an age of 'rebirth' throughout Europe with discoveries and advances in medicine and science (Copernicus, Fallopius, Leonardo da Vinci), architecture and art (Botticelli, Brueghel, Michelangelo, Titian), literature (Caxton, Dante, Shakespeare), and exploration (Columbus, Drake, Magellan, Vasco da Gama).

★ In Italy, composers of religious music were exploiting the resonant acoustics of the great churches, including St Peter's in Rome and St Mark's in Venice.

★ Religious music was often very elaborate. Many voices sang overlapping melodies, creating a seamless blend of ethereal sounds, which almost rendered the words indistinguishable. This technique of writing many overlapping parts is called polyphony (many sounding). In contrast, the technique of antiphony (sounding against) produced a different texture by bouncing single words or phrases from one part of the choir to another. Both techniques of writing were wonderfully effective in resonant churches.

★ Music flourished outside the church too. Town and city corporations set up bands to play at civic functions, and in the countryside, villagers had their own songs and dances. The first printed music appeared in the second half of the 15th century.

★ In England in early Tudor times, the hall was the setting for banquets and dancing in wealthy households with the musicians playing in the minstrels' gallery. Dancing was an important part of this upper class social life and many styles, emerging in different countries, became popular throughout Europe. The estampie (page 10) had set the pattern for partner dances, and now most dances were variations of the same basic steps.

★ During the Tudor period these 'court' dances had divided into two types – elegant, walking dances for the older guests, and lively, energetic dances for the younger.

★ By the time of Henry VIII in later Tudor times, visitors were often received in the comfort of the privy chamber and the musicians adapted to this more intimate arrangement accordingly. They tended to play in adjoining rooms with open doors and often scaled down the number of players as necessary. The gradual disuse of the halls in favour of this type of smaller-scale entertainment spread across Europe.

★ There was a great increase in the composition and publication of instrumental music, particularly for the middle classes to play in their own homes.

★ Instruments were often played together in families of the same type, known as consorts. For example, many homes would have a chest of viols (string instruments which predate the modern string family stored in a chest), or recorders, which they would play, sitting around a table, from specially printed music which allowed all players to read the music at once.

Renaissance Pueri concinite

WHAT YOU NEED TO KNOW ABOUT PUERI CONCINITE

Composer: Jacob Handl (1550–1591)

★ Handl was a Cistercian monk who travelled the monasteries of Eastern Europe as a composer and choirmaster in order to develop his music.

★ Many European composers were inspired by musical developments in Italy, and adapted these developments to their own compositions. Handl's vocal music is said to have been influenced by the composers Andrea and Giovanni Gabrieli, who made a huge impact on the musical and religious world with the scale and magnificence of their work at St Mark's in Venice during the second half of the 16th century.

Features of the music

★ *Pueri concinite* is for four unaccompanied male voices: two trebles (high), one alto (upper middle) and one tenor (lower middle). The Latin text celebrates the birth of Christ. Handl incorporates a lilting 15th century German carol melody (*Joseph dearest, Joseph mine*) on the words 'quod divina voluit clementia'.

★ Handl skilfully uses contrasting textures (ways of combining sounds) in this short piece to provide colour and interest, and to reinforce the meaning of the words. The musical terms for these textures are homophony, polyphony and antiphony, but they have been given simpler names for the purposes of the activities:

- **blocks** (homophony) – voices singing the same words together, used here to emphasise celebrating in unity;

- **relays** (polyphony) – separately-moving, overlapping voices, used here to give a joyful impression of many voices raised in individual praise;

- **ping pong** (antiphony) – different voices bounce words back and forth, used here to show excitement.

ABOUT THE ACTIVITIES

Listen to *Pueri concinite* – the class listens to the music, focussing on the voices and how they combine.

Blocks, relays and ping pong – singing a simple melody (used in *Pueri concinite*) using three textures.

Sing a song to celebrate performance – making a whole class performance of a song using three textures.

Listen to *Pueri concinite* – listening and detecting the order of three vocal textures.

Instrumental blocks – starting with blocks, the class prepare an instrumental piece based on the three vocal textures.

Instrumental relays and ping pong – continuing the transfer of vocal textures to instruments in the preparation of a class instrumental piece.

Perform instrumental textures – structuring and performing the class instrumental piece.

Listen to Pueri concinite

Explain that this music is performed by four male singers: two high voices, one medium and one lower.

Questions you might ask

- Do the voices sing in unison – all together? (No; sometimes you can hear them singing alone; sometimes together; sometimes one after the other.)

Blocks, relays and ping pong

1. Teach everyone this melody, track 11 (WB2):

F		G	A		Bb	C'		Bb	A		G	F		G	A		
Sing		a	song		to	ce	-	le-brate			at	Christ-	mas	time		

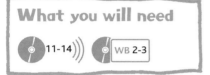
2. Blocks – sing the melody three times without a break (track 12, WB3):

> Sing a song to celebrate at Christmas time

> Sing a song to celebrate at Christmas time

> Sing a song to celebrate at Christmas time

3. Relays – divide into three groups and sing the melody with one group starting after another and overlapping (track 13, WB3):

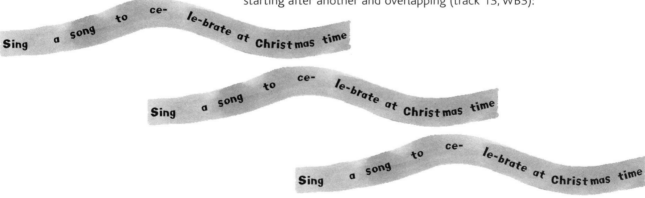

Sing a song to ce-le-brate at Christmas time

Sing a song to ce-le-brate at Christmas time

Sing a song to ce-le-brate at Christmas time

4. Ping pong – still in their groups, ask the class to suggest single words to bounce from one group to another. Think about the notes to sing, a rhythm and an order (eg track 14, WB3):

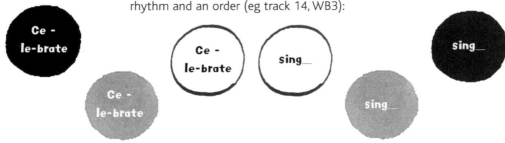

Ce-le-brate   Ce-le-brate   sing   sing

Ce-le-brate   sing

Renaissance Pueri conciniti

Sing a song to celebrate performance

What you will need

11-14))) WB 4

1. Remind the children of the graphics used to show the textures they practised when they sang 'Sing a song to celebrate at Christmas time'.

2. Together, work out a performance of the song in the order shown in the graphics (WB4):

Listen to Pueri concinite

What you will need

10))) WB1/5-6

Read the Latin text and its translation to the children (WB1). After listening to track 10 as many times as needed, decide the order in which the textures are being used in the piece (WB5).

Questions you might ask

• Can you identify any similarities between this music and ours? (The textures are those we used in our piece; we heard our melody in it.)

• Which textures do you recognise? (Blocks, relays, ping pong.)

• In which order do you hear them sung? (The chart on WB6 reveals the order in which the textures are heard.)

Instrumental blocks

What you will need

WB 7

1. Explain that the children are going to transfer the vocal textures to instruments, starting with blocks.

2. Remind them of the melody 'Sing a song to celebrate at Christmas time'. Clap the rhythm of the words:

Sing   a song   to ce - le-brate   at Christ - mas time

• A selection of untuned instruments – one per child, eg

3. Give a small group of volunteers untuned instruments and ask them to play the rhythm as you clap together again.

4. Now try playing the melody as well on a tuned percussion instrument:

F		G	A		Bb	C'		Bb	A		G	F		G	A		
Sing		a	song		to	ce	-	le-brate			at	Christ -		mas time		

• Tuned notes – F G A Bb C':

5. Select a third of the class to continue working with a selection of instruments and copies of the Blocks worksheet (WB7).

• One or more copies of the Blocks worksheet (WB7).

Instrumental relays and ping pong

I. Divide into two groups and perform 'Sing a song to celebrate at Christmas time' together in relays, clapping the rhythm of the words at the same time. When this is secure, perform it again, singing in your heads, while clapping out loud. Transfer the performance to untuned instruments.

2. Give one volunteer per relay group a tuned instrument and ask them to play the melody for their group as you sing and clap/play again:

F		G	A		Bb	C'		Bb	A		G	F		G	A		
🎵		🎵	🎵		🎵	🎵		🎵	🎵		🎵	🎵		🎵	🎵		
Sing		a	song		to	ce	-	le-	brate		at	Christ	-	mas	time		

F		G	A		Bb	C'		Bb	A		G	F		G	A		
🎵		🎵	🎵		🎵	🎵		🎵	🎵		🎵	🎵		🎵	🎵		
Sing		a	song		to	ce	-	le-	brate		at	Christ	-	mas	time		

3. Leave one of the groups to continue working on their relay music with a selection of instruments and copies of the Relays worksheet (WB8).

4. Help the remaining group to get started with the Ping pong texture using these word rhythms and notes from the song (WB9):

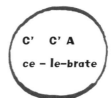

Perform Instrumental textures

I. When the groups have had time to complete their arrangements, listen to each separately. Are there any problems to solve, eg are the separate relay parts clear?

2. Now structure the sections into a class piece:

– ask the children to suggest different orders for the groups to play in;

– listen to and then discuss their preferences. (Note: the individual group pieces will not necessarily be performed at the same speed – do the children think this should affect their decisions?)

– discuss and decide in which order to play the three sections.

3. Draw a plan of the final class piece (individual children may draw plans of their favourite order as well) eg

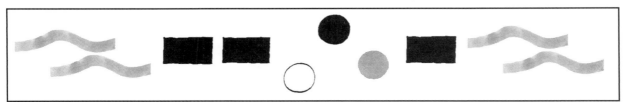

Renaissance Martin said to his man

WHAT YOU NEED TO KNOW ABOUT MARTIN SAID TO HIS MAN
Composer: Thomas Ravenscroft (1590–c1635)

★ This song was published by Ravenscroft in 1609 in a collection of three- and four-part songs and rounds, *Deuteromelia*. Most of the songs are settings of humorous and popular poems including the first known printing of *Three blind mice*.

★ Although Ravenscroft was a learned church musician and music theorist, he was determined to write music for all tastes: for 'court, city and country'.

★ This four-part drinking song is sung in folk clubs to this day. Singers make up their own nonsense words to it.

Features of the music

★ This tavern song describes the impossible visions of one who has 'well drunken'. It is composed for four voices: soprano (high), alto (upper middle), tenor (lower middle) and bass (low). After the first verse and chorus each singer has a chance to make up new words, while the others sing the repeated chorus lines.

ABOUT THE ACTIVITIES

Singing *Martin said to his man* – the class learn the song thoroughly.

Adding new words – pairs of children make up new words to the song.

Listen to *Martin said to his man* – recognising the similarities and differences between Ravenscroft's version of the song and the one the children have sung.

Singing Martin said to his man

1. Teach the first verse and chorus, track 15 (WB10). Listen several times, and join in on the chorus lines. When secure, sing the verse lines as well:

> **Martin said to his man,** *(verse)*
>   **Fie, man, fie!** *(chorus)*
> **Martin said to his man,**
>   **Who's the fool now?**
> **Martin said to his man,**
>   **'Fill thou the cup and I the can.'**
>   **Thou hast well drunken, man,**
>   **Who's the fool now?**
>   **Thou hast well drunken, man,**
>   **Who's the fool now?**

Teaching tip
When you sing without the support of the CD, give the children a clear direction of when to start and at what speed – as demonstrated on the recording.

2. Teach the other verses in the same way. Notice how each new verse contains two nonsensical happenings, eg

> **I saw a goose ring a hog...**
> **...And the snail bite a dog.**

3. When the song is confident and clear, with and without the recording, ask individuals to sing the verse lines and the others to sing the chorus lines.

Adding new words

1. In pairs, the children make up a new verse from two nonsensical happenings. Can they make the two new lines rhyme? eg:

... I saw an ant eat a whale and a supersonic snail...

... I saw a web spin a spider and an apple drinking cider...

... I saw a chicken chase a fox and a Jack jump in a box...

2. Sing the song with the new verses. Each pair sings their own verse, either together or one line each, and all join in with the chorus.

Listen to Martin said to his man

Questions you might ask

• What are the similarities and differences between this song and our version? (It is the same song; neither uses instruments; the singers take turns to sing alone; in this music the voices sing different parts, while we all sing the same melody together.)

Renaissance Mistress Winter's jump

WHAT YOU NEED TO KNOW ABOUT MISTRESS WINTER'S JUMP
Composer: John Dowland (1563–1626)

★ Dowland wished to be appointed as a court musician to Elizabeth I in 1594. He was unsuccessful, probably because he was a Catholic during a time when royalty favoured Protestantism. He was a highly-skilled lute player and singer and was famed for his performances throughout Europe. Many of his compositions survive in manuscript and a few were printed. They show him to be one of the most gifted composers of the period. He wrote collections of songs and many pieces for lute. In 1612 he achieved his ambition and became lutenist to the court of James I.

Features of the music

★ This energetic dance is based on a pattern of eight counts. The dance melody is in two repeated sections:

Section 1	Repeat	Section 2		Repeat	
A	**A**	**B¹**	**B²**	**B¹**	**B²**
1-8	1-8	1-8	1-8	1-8	1-8

★ The dance is played twice on this recording:

1st time: violin plays the melody, accompanied by bass viol, guitar, lute and mandora (a small high-pitched lute often played with a plectrum). Listen out for the decorations (improvised embellishments) played on the mandora.

2nd time: the violin repeats the melody; the mandora has an even more decorative part.

ABOUT THE ACTIVITIES

Listen to *Mistress Winter's jump* – focussing on the instruments and the structure of the music.

Performing *Mistress Winter's jump* – learning a dance based on authentic steps of the period, which give an idea of the stepping and jumping dance which may have been performed by Mistress Winter herself.

★ The piece begins and ends with a reverence – one long-sounding chord played while the dancers bow.

Features of the dance

simple forward   double forward

★ Many popular dances of the time were based on two steps: the simple and the double, performed either stepping forwards or backwards. This diagram shows you the steps moving forward (count to four).

★ Pairs of dancers would begin by facing the host and hostess, or if they themselves were dancing, the place in the hall where they sat. The B1 parts of the dance give the opportunity for each couple to make up steps or 'tricks' according to the Elizabethan fashion of improvising fancy, athletic steps as additions to the basic dance.

Listen to Mistress Winter's jump

Use WB13 to show the children the instruments which they hear as they listen and to familiarise them with the structure of the music.

Questions you might ask

- How many sections are there? (Two main sections, which are each repeated.)
- Do you recognise the instrument playing the melody? (Violin.)
- One of the other instruments – the mandora – also plays the melody, but a much more complicated version of it with extra notes and very fast, skilful playing. What are these variations called? (Decorations.)

Performing Mistress Winter's jump

1. Show the children the diagram of the dance and notice together how there are eight steps to each section.

2. Remind the children of the reverence which begins and ends the music, and in pairs practise the reverence with and without the music:

   – each pair hold hands – boy's right palm upwards with thumb curled over girl's left palm resting on top; both look ahead;

   – girl bends knees slightly and rises slowly;

   – at the same time, boy removes 'hat' and sweeps left arm down to side while stepping back on right foot and bending right knee. Left leg stretched in front.

3. Now teach one section at a time without the music then with the track for that section, in which the steps are called (WB14).

4. Finally perform the dance to track 17. Arrange the pairs in a block facing forward. All the pairs will move forward slightly during B2.

What you will need

Teaching tips
Encourage the children to look ahead, taking small, neat steps no more than a foot's length for good balance and elegance.
Check that everyone can step accurately, show good balance, and move neatly but not stiffly in time to the music.

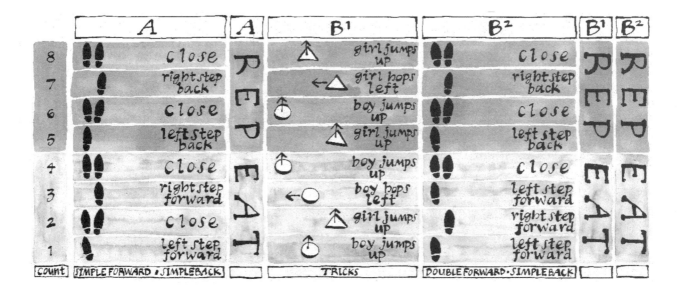

count	A		A	B¹		B²		B¹	B²
8		close		girl jumps up			close		
7		right step back	R	girl hops left			right step back	R	R
6		close	E	boy jumps up			close	E	E
5		left step back	P	girl jumps up			left step back	P	P
4		close	E	boy jumps up			close	E	E
3		right step forward	A	boy hops left			left step forward	A	A
2		close	T	girl jumps up			right step forward		T
1		left step forward		boy jumps up			left step forward		

| count | SIMPLE FORWARD · SIMPLE BACK | | TRICKS | DOUBLE FORWARD · SIMPLE BACK | |

Renaissance links

WHAT YOU NEED TO KNOW ABOUT THE MUSIC

Three further pieces give the opportunity for the children to hear more examples of musical instruments from the Renaissance period:

– a popular tune arranged for performance out of doors on drum and shawm;

– a piece of court music played on chamber organ;

– a courtly dance played by a consort of lutes.

Packington's pound
Composer: anon (16th century)

Packington's pound was one of the most popular Elizabethan tunes. It was reused again and again in songs and instrumental pieces. This version is arranged for the outdoors, perhaps to play on a street corner or in a slow procession. The loud shawm, which plays the melody, and the drum would have quickly summoned up a crowd to gather round and listen.

The piece is in three sections. The first (played twice) and last have almost the same rhythm but the melody is altered. The middle section is different in rhythm and melody.

In nomine
Composer: Richard Alwood (mid 16th century)

This piece is for chamber organ – a small, portable instrument, often used for secular music during the Renaissance. It would have been played to the patron and guests as they ate in their private apartments. Alwood, like many composers of his time, uses a pre-existing melody, in this case a plainchant (see page 5), as the basis around which to weave new melodies. The slow plainchant is hardly noticeable. A new, fast, three-note rising melody overlaps many times in higher and lower-sounding parts of the keyboard.

Suzanna
Composer: John Dowland (1563–1626)

This lilting, three-beat piece for dancing or listening to is played by a consort (page 15) of lutes – two lutes and a theorbo (a bass lute). In performance, Dowland and his contemporaries often improvised skilfully on simple melodies. This piece gives an idea of the way they added decorations.

ASSESSMENT GUIDANCE

★ Can the children recognise and explain how music can be organised in a variety of different textures?

★ Can they perform and compose music which has a variety of different textures?

★ Can they sing, pitching accurately and linking expression with the style of the song?

★ Can they describe, compare and evaluate different kinds of music using appropriate musical vocabulary?

★ Do they respond to music using movement and dance?

★ Can they talk about the context and purpose of a range of music?

ABOUT THE ACTIVITIES

This section enables the children to work independently with three pieces of music which have links to things they have heard and learned during the earlier activities.

What you will need
19))) — WB 15

Shawm

What you will need
20))) — WB 16

What you will need
21))) — WB 17

Theorbo

Baroque introduction

WHAT YOU NEED TO KNOW ABOUT THE BAROQUE PERIOD

★ The term 'baroque' comes from the Portuguese word 'barocco' meaning encrusted, or rough, pearl. It was originally used in a derogatory way by critics of the elaborately decorated music of the time. Both architecture and music became more dramatic and ornate.

★ A great expansion of instrumental music and new musical structures took place during this time.

★ Two modes (page 5) were being used more and more and came to be known as the major and minor keys, while the other modes fell into disuse. The pattern of notes in a major or minor scale is always the same, whatever the starting note – a major scale starting on C (C D E F G A B C') sounds the same – but a little higher in pitch – if the starting note is D (D E F♯ G A B C♯' D'). Composers could now move from one key to another within one piece of music. Baroque composers explored and established all the major and minor keys and the colourful relationships between them.

★ The harpsichord was developed during the 15th century. Its strings are plucked by tiny splinters of quill in a mechanism operated from the keyboard. It remained a popular household instrument until the end of the 18th century – a four hundred year period. Throughout the baroque period it played a key role in ensemble music of all kinds, and its repertoire of solo music was greatly expanded.

★ The baroque orchestra consisted mainly of string instruments of the violin family (violin, viola, cello and bass), which had replaced the viols in popularity. Sometimes a small number of woodwind or brass instruments were added.

★ A feature that was always present was the continuo part. This was performed by a small section of the orchestra playing the bass line of the music. A keyboard instrument, such as organ or harpsichord, was used to fill out the harmonies above the bass line. The keyboard player read from 'figured bass' - a number notation added to the written bass line. This suggested the chords to be played but allowed for personal interpretation by the performer, who was expected to improvise skilfully and appropriately. The continuo section gave a very strong lead to the other musicians and the keyboard player, rather than a conductor, often directed the whole orchestra.

★ Vocal music, both secular and religious, also flourished. Following the Reformation, religious music was no longer restricted to Latin texts. Composers used their local languages to aid the congregation's understanding of the service. One of the many forms used was the cantata (sung piece), a collection of solos, duets and choruses for voices and chamber orchestra.

Baroque Chiacona

WHAT YOU NEED TO KNOW ABOUT CHIACONA
Composer: Tarquinio Merula (1594–1665)

✦ Little is known of Merula's life, except for the information given on the title pages of his surviving compositions. He was an Italian church organist and court composer, and published several collections of church and secular music.

Features of the music

✦ The chaconne (the French spelling is commonly used) was originally a dance, which became a popular structure for instrumental music. A chaconne contains a ground bass – a repeating pattern of notes played by the lowest-sounding instrument in a group. The ground bass provides a simple foundation over which the other players perform other melodies and decorations.

✦ This chaconne comprises the ground bass played by harpsichord and bass sackbut, over which two cornetts play first a melody then an impressive series of florid decorations. Players were expected to be able to improvise freely on the music written by the composer, and this chaconne shows off the virtuosity of the two cornett players who play the decorations. As well as playing the ground bass, the harpsichord plays a continuo accompaniment (page 25), which holds the whole effect together:

- the ground bass is heard alone first;
- the cornetts then play a simple melody over it;
- next the two cornett players perform a series of very rapid and ornate embellishments – decorations – over the ground bass. They feature:

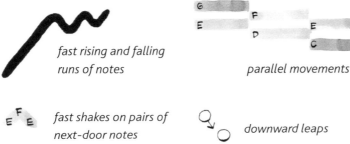

fast rising and falling runs of notes

parallel movements

fast shakes on pairs of next-door notes

downward leaps

✦ Sackbut
The forerunner of the modern trombone, a sackbut has a slide mechanism to alter the length of its metal tubing, and thus alter the pitch of the sounds it can produce. Sackbuts of different sizes were often played together in groups and were combined with cornetts in church and royal bands.

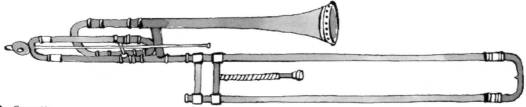

✦ Cornett
This is a wind instrument made of leather-covered wood with finger holes similar to those of a recorder, but with a small cup-shaped mouthpiece like that of a brass instrument. It was used for all kinds of outdoor and indoor music throughout this period.

ABOUT THE ACTIVITIES

Ground bass game – the children learn to clap the rhythm of the ground bass, then individually make up new rhythms on body percussion to 'decorate' it. The aim is to develop the skill of making two patterns fit together.

Listen to ground bass and melody – noticing the ground bass rhythm now played on harpsichord followed by the cornett playing a melody.

Play *Chiacona* ground bass and melody – transferring the ground bass and melody to tuned percussion.

Listen to *Chiacona* decorations – recognising the different types of decorations played by the cornetts.

Play *Chiacona* decorations – transferring the decorations to tuned percussion and making up new decorations.

Listen to *Chiacona* – hearing the complete piece performed and recognising how it is structured.

Perform *Chiacona* – refining and then performing **Chiacona**.

What you will need

 22-24)))  WB 1-3*

*Whiteboard display numberings begin again from 1.

Ground bass game

1. Teach the ground bass rhythm, track 22 (WB1). Give a count in of **10, 11** to start. All count the beat steadily and clap the pattern, which begins on the 12th beat. Repeat it several times until it is secure:

2. Next, all clap the rhythm, but count the beat silently in your heads (take care not to let the clapping get gradually faster).

3. Divide into two groups. Group 1 counts silently and claps. Group 2 adds this new rhythm, eg track 23 (WB2):

4. Form a circle. In turns, each child makes up a new body percussion rhythm and performs it during one cycle of the ground bass, which the others continue to clap, eg track 24 (WB3):

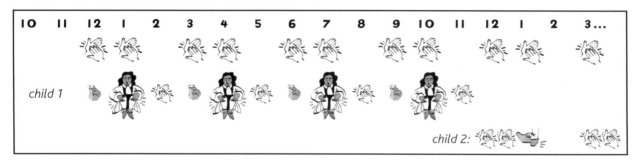

Does each pattern follow on smoothly from the one before?

Listen to the ground bass and melody

What you will need

 25))) WB 4

In track 25 (WB4), the children hear a harpsichord playing the rhythm they have clapped, then they hear a cornett adding a melody.

Questions you might ask

- What do you notice about the music which the harpsichord plays? (It has the same rhythm as the clapping pattern we learnt; the clapping pattern has a tune; the tune is played on the low notes of the harpsichord.)

- What do you notice about the music the cornett plays? (It plays a tune; the tune lasts the same amount of time as the harpsichord tune; the tunes fit together.)

Baroque Chiacona

Play Chiacona ground bass and melody

1. Invite a volunteer to play the ground bass on an instrument while the others count and clap as before, eg track 26 (WB5):

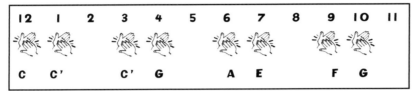

Play it over and over again without stopping.

2. Divide into pairs, each with a tuned instrument, to learn how to play the ground bass. Play along with track 26 or WB5 if you like.

3. When everyone is secure with the ground bass, learn the cornett melody:

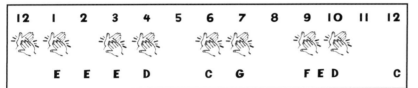

The melody starts on beat 1 and ends on beat 12. Keep repeating it on your own or play along with the recording on track 27 (WB5).

4. If the pairs can confidently play the ground bass and the melody, they may try combining them. One child plays the ground bass while the other plays the melody. Keep repeating until secure then swap parts.

Listen to Chiacona decorations

On tracks 28-31 (WB6), the children hear the cornett making up decorations to play along with the ground bass.

Questions you might ask

- If we give the decorations these names – scales, parallels, leaps, shakes – which track is which? (Track 28 scales, track 29 shakes, track 30 leaps, track 31 parallels.)

- Do you think the names suit the decorations? Why?

Play Chiacona decorations

1. Still in pairs, the children make up shakes, scales, leaps and parallels in any way they like. Try out different sequences and combinations of notes. Practise the ideas first on their own, then with each partner playing the ground bass. Revise if necessary and swap parts. (They may if they wish play along with track 32, WB7.)

2. Each pair decides on a final version of their music then plays it to the class.

What you will need

🔊 26-27))) 💿 WB 5

- a tuned instrument each, or to share, with these notes:

Teaching tips

Remind the children to keep a steady beat as they play and to keep counting quietly out loud or in their heads.

Listen to or play along with tracks 26-27, WB5 whenever the children need more support in checking the accuracy of their performance.

What you will need

🔊 28-31))) 💿 WB 6

What you will need

🔊 32))) 💿 WB 7

- A tuned instrument each, or to share, with these notes:

What you will need

 33)))  WB 8

Listen to Chiacona

Explain that this is the complete *Chiacona* from which the children have used ideas to create their own chiacona ground bass and decorations.

Ask them to notice the ground bass and the melody and to hear if they can recognise these decorations when they appear in the music (WB8):

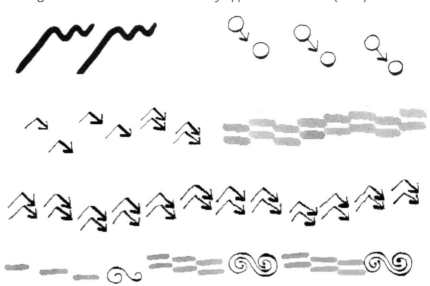

Questions you might ask

- How is this piece similar to yours? (We played the same ground bass and melody; we used the same type of decorations.)

- Which of the decorations that you used can you recognise in this music?

- How does the composer use the two cornetts? (They take turns; play together; copy one another. Their decorations are very fast and exciting.)

- When you listen again, notice the bass sackbut playing all the way through. Can you hear what it plays? (Mostly it plays the ground bass; in the middle of the piece it stops and plays a long melody which moves up and down.)

Perform Chiacona

1. Give the pairs opportunities to refine their work after listening to Merula's *Chiacona*. Are there any parts they would like to add or change?

2. Ask them to decide on a final version to perform to the class.

What you will need

 WB 5/8

Teaching tip
Are the pairs able to keep the ground bass going steadily? Have they chosen and ordered their decorations with care and deliberation?

Baroque Sonata for harpsichord

WHAT YOU NEED TO KNOW ABOUT THE MUSIC

Composer: Domenico Scarlatti (1685–1757)

★ Scarlatti belonged to a very musical Italian family. He first learned to play the organ and harpsichord with his father, Alessandro, who was a successful composer and music teacher. He became a friend of Handel, when they met in Venice in 1708, and in a contest to discover which of the two was the better keyboard player, the general opinion was that Handel slightly excelled as an organist, but as a harpsichordist, Scarlatti was his equal.

★ In 1729, Scarlatti was appointed to the Spanish court where, towards the end of his life, he composed an incredible 555 sonatas for harpsichord.

★ The term sonata (sound piece) had earlier been loosely applied to any instrumental music, large scale or small. Now it described a piece for a solo instrument or a small group. Scarlatti possessed an extraordinary inventiveness. Though he changed the overall structure of his sonatas very little, each was in detail unique.

Features of the music

★ Most of his sonatas have only a single, unbroken movement containing two contrasting sections (binary structure, A B). This one, unusually, has a third section very similar to the first (ternary structure, A B A).

★ Listen out for the higher and lower parts played by the right and left hands respectively – they play almost equal roles in the musical interest.

A is in the major key (giving a bright, cheerful mood):
– lively falling then rising patterns played by both hands moving in parallel; trills (quickly alternated adjacent notes) are added for decoration;
– falling sequences of skipping rhythms in the lower part;
– downward leaps in the lower part and wide upward leaps in the upper part;
– the lower part's skipping rhythm is combined with the upper part moving two notes apart in parallel.

B is in the minor key (giving a more sombre mood):
– short, falling melodies are repeated;
– an exciting build-up of notes played together leads to:
– a very fast falling run of notes – a scale.

A returns in the major key with some small changes.

ABOUT THE ACTIVITIES

Dominoes – pairs or small groups of children will investigate binary structure (A B), composing short pieces of music focussing on the musical elements. Later they will extend their pieces into ternary structure (A B A).

Listen to *Sonata for harpsichord* – noticing how Scarlatti organises the sections of his music into A B A, ternary form.

What you will need

 34-35))) WB 9-16

- A set of domino cards for each group:

- A variety of instruments with a range of sounds:

- Copies of the blank ternary card (WB16).

Teaching tip

Extend the activity by asking the groups to think of new contrasts to use as the basis of their A B A music, eg pluck/blow/pluck; black keys/white keys/black keys.

What you will need

 36))) WB 17

Dominoes

1. Discuss the cards and what they show (*contrasts within elements such as duration, dynamics, tempo, pitch, etc*). Listen to the musical examples on track 34 and decide which dominoes they match (WB9-12). Explain the term binary – the term for music in two contrasting sections, A and B.

2. Divide the class into pairs or small groups. Give each a set of domino cards (WB13) and access to a range of different-sounding instruments.

3. Each group chooses one domino card and composes a short piece of music with two sections, A and B, corresponding to the contrasts on the card, eg

Encourage each group to think carefully about the instruments they choose – the aim is to make what is on the domino clear to the listeners.

Give the groups turns to play their music to the others. Can the rest of the class identify each group's domino and the elements used?

4. Next, ask the children to develop their music by using two dominoes simultaneously (WB14), eg

Again, the groups play to the others, who identify the matching dominoes.

5. Listen to the musical example on track 35 (WB15) and explain the term ternary form – A B A. Give each group a blank triple domino card (WB16), on which to record their chosen contrasts. Explain that the final A section does not have to be identical to the first but should be very similar.

Listen to Sonata for harpsichord

Questions you might ask

- What are your first impressions of this piece?

- Did you notice how the piece is organised? (It has three sections, the first section returns at the end. It is in ternary form, A B A.)

- Can you describe the way the music changes in the middle of the piece? (There is a long pattern of notes from high to low (a descending scale) followed by a pause.)

Baroque Recorder concerto

WHAT YOU NEED TO KNOW ABOUT THE MUSIC
Composer: Antonio Vivaldi (1678–1741)

★ Vivaldi was one of the most important composers of the baroque period. He was nicknamed the 'Red Priest' because of his red hair and because he trained as a priest. He composed over 360 concertos for solo instrument and orchestra. Many of his compositions featured his own instrument, the violin, but he wrote concertos for many other instruments, including this one for treble recorder.

Features of the music

★ Vivaldi wrote this as a chamber concerto, meaning that it was for a small group of instruments – a treble recorder (the solo instrument), two violins, one cello and a harpsichord.

★ There are three movements in all; the first and last are at a lively tempo (allegro) and the middle movement featured here is slow (largo). The minor key of the music along with the slow pace gives the second movement a melancholy but lyrical mood.

★ Accompaniment pattern

– the harpsichord and cello play the continuo and set the speed by playing on each beat to a slow count of three (track 37):

1   2   3   1   2   3   etc

– the two violins add rising and falling patterns.

This accompaniment pattern continues throughout.

★ Solo recorder

– after the accompaniment pattern is heard on its own, the solo recorder begins a slow, flowing melody.

– long, smooth phrases are decorated with:

fast, rising runs of notes;
trills (next-door notes rapidly alternated).

ABOUT THE ACTIVITIES

Listen to *Recorder concerto* – noticing the accompaniment pattern.

Concerto dance: group – devising dance movements to perform for the accompaniment pattern, reflecting the structure and mood of the music.

Listen to *Recorder concerto* – noticing the solo recorder.

Concerto dance: solo – improvising dance movements to perform to the solo recorder music, reflecting the structure and mood of the music. Finally the groups and soloists combine their dance movements.

solo recorder

cello and harpsichord continuo

violins

What you will need

Listen to Recorder concerto

Ask the children to focus their listening on the accompaniment instruments.

Questions you might ask

- What do you notice about the music these instruments play? (It is slow and regular; it doesn't change; the violins play a rising and falling pattern which keeps repeating; the harpsichord and cello play steadily on the main beat:

  1   2   3   1   2   3.)

What you will need

- Space to move, eg a hall.

Concerto dance: group

1. Play track 38 (WB19), asking the children to try out some simple movements to perform in a circle on the main beat, eg

   – facing around the circle take three forward steps on counts 1 2 3;
   – curtsy or bow to the centre for three counts;
   – repeat all then turn and step back the other way.

2. Ask individual children to demonstrate and discuss their ideas. Which do they think match the music most closely?

3. Divide the class into circles of five or six. Each circle devises a set of movements to perform during the music.

Listen to Recorder concerto

Ask the children to focus their listening on the solo recorder.

What you will need

Questions you might ask

- What do you notice about the recorder melody? (It is smooth. It does not repeat in a pattern. It is mostly slow but there are some fast decorations. It uses low and high notes, sometimes moving higher very quickly.)

Concerto dance: solo

What you will need

- Space to move, eg a hall.

1. One child per group, listening carefully to the recorder melody (track 39, WB21), improvises movements which reflect the shapes of the music, eg

   – lead up and down with alternate hands, elbows, arms;
   – turn at different speeds, responding to the music;
   – flutter hands to match shakes and trills.

2. Combine the group and solo dances (track 37, WB22). Each soloist dances in the centre of the circle. While the accompaniment group performs its circle dance, the soloist improvises a freer dance, responding to the recorder melody.

Baroque links

WHAT YOU NEED TO KNOW ABOUT THE MUSIC

The three pieces in this section provide further listening examples which link closely with the music the children have worked on in depth:

- a piece by Samuel Scheidt for cornetts and sackbuts, instruments already heard in the *Chiacona*;

- extracts from the first and third movements of Vivaldi's *Recorder Concerto*;

- a chorus for voices and small Baroque orchestra in which the children can identify the musical textures.

Canzona super entrada aechiopicam
Composer: Samuel Scheidt (1587–1654)

A canzona was originally a song for several voices, but in the 16th and 17th centuries it became a popular instrumental form featuring overlapping melodies and imitation (one instrument copying another).

This canzona for two cornetts and four sackbuts with a chamber organ continuo (hardly noticeable) is based on an old popular melody. It is played first by one cornett, imitated at a higher pitch by second cornett, at a lower pitch by the sackbut, then by the even lower bass sackbut. Inbetween, the instruments overlap in a seamless texture.

Recorder concerto
Composer: Antonio Vivaldi (1678–1741)

The first and last movements of the *Recorder concerto* are fast (allegro) in contrast with the slow (largo) middle movement. The harpsichord and cello play a continuo accompaniment while the recorder and two violins play as though in a lively conversation.

Chorus from The hunt cantata
Composer: Johann Sebastian Bach (1685–1750)

Cantatas (sung pieces) were one of the many religious and secular forms of vocal music of the period; they were collections of solos, duets and choruses for voices and chamber orchestra.

This is from one of Bach's secular cantatas, composed to celebrate the birthday of a Duke, a keen huntsman, at the court where Bach was employed. The singers are two sopranos (high female), tenor (high male) and bass (low male). They enter in turn from the highest to lowest voice with the first melody – an upward leap followed by a falling run of notes. The small orchestra of strings, oboes, bassoon and harpsichord then repeat this treatment of the melody, and horns add decoration and a hunting atmosphere.

ASSESSMENT GUIDANCE

★ Can the children maintain repeating rhythmic and melodic patterns (ostinati)?

★ Can they improvise rhythmic phrases, keeping a steady beat?

★ Can they improvise melodic phrases, using a scale as a base?

★ Can they compose music using devices such as ground bass (melodic ostinato), melody and decoration?

★ Can the children recognise and develop ideas using musical structures, eg binary (A B) and ternary (A B A)?

★ Can they listen to music and use correct musical vocabulary to describe its texture, structure and metre?

ABOUT THE ACTIVITIES

This section enables the children to work independently with three pieces of music which have links to things they have heard and learned during the earlier activities.

What you will need
 40 WB 23

What you will need
 41 WB 24

What you will need
42 WB 25

Bach

Classical introduction

WHAT YOU NEED TO KNOW ABOUT THE CLASSICAL PERIOD

★ The elaborately-decorated buildings and music of the baroque period were gradually followed by the much simpler and clearer designs of the classical period. The emphasis in architecture and music during the 18th century was on grace and beauty, balanced proportions and formal structure. In all kinds of music, strong melody lines became the outstanding feature.

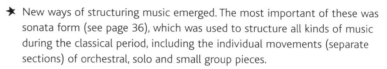
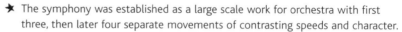

★ New ways of structuring music emerged. The most important of these was sonata form (see page 36), which was used to structure all kinds of music during the classical period, including the individual movements (separate sections) of orchestral, solo and small group pieces.

★ The symphony was established as a large scale work for orchestra with first three, then later four separate movements of contrasting speeds and character.

★ The orchestra expanded in size and range of instruments during this time, particularly in the woodwind section which now began to include the newly-invented clarinet. In addition to a larger string section, the classical orchestra frequently combined flutes, oboes, bassoons and horns. As the orchestra grew in strength, the use of the harpsichord continuo as a supporting background gradually stopped.

★ Classical composers wrote vocal music for the church, but opera held a greater fascination. The elaborate staging and special effects of earlier operas became less important than dramatic content as composers developed characters and plots to comment on aspects of human nature.

★ In England, the 17th century Puritans had regarded Christmas as superstition, and their continuing influence meant that from 1700 to 1782 the only Christmas carol accepted by the Church of England was 'While shepherds watched'. There remains, however, a wealth of carols from the Non-conformist repertoire.

Classical The 'hen' symphony (1st movement)

WHAT YOU NEED TO KNOW ABOUT THE 'HEN' SYMPHONY

Composer: Joseph Haydn (1732–1809)

★ Haydn's father was a wheelwright, but Haydn had already shown a talent for music by the time he was eight, when the organist of Vienna's cathedral heard him sing and recruited him into the choir. Later, he became director of music for the Prince of Esterhazy and his family. During the thirty years he stayed with them, his enormous output of music was published and his reputation spread throughout Europe.

Features of the music

★ **The 'hen' symphony** (composed in 1785) is one of over a hundred symphonies Haydn composed. By the end of the classical period the organisation of a symphony into four contrasting movements had become standard, and Haydn's selection of movements for this one was typical of the time. He marked them:

1. Allegro (fast)
2. Andante (slow)
3. Menuet (a dance)
4. Vivace (fast)

★ This symphony is one of Haydn's six 'Paris symphonies', commissioned for a Parisian orchestra. It was nicknamed 'La poule' (the hen) because of the clucking oboe part in the first movement. The orchestra contains:

  – 1 flute;
  – 2 oboes;
  – 2 bassoons;
  – 2 horns;
  – strings (violins, violas, cellos, double basses).

★ The first movement is in a structure called sonata form, which has clearly identifiable sections:

– Exposition
  The composer presents (exposits) the musical ideas on which the whole movement is based. They are grouped within a first subject followed by a second subject.

– Development
  The musical ideas of the exposition are developed.

– Recapitulation
  The exposition is played again (recapitulated).

– Coda – ending.

oboe

ABOUT THE ACTIVITIES

Hen chant exposition – the children learn then perform a rhythmic chant based on the six musical ideas Haydn used for his first and second subjects. The chant forms the exposition of a new piece in sonata form which they will create. Six groups perform one idea each.

Hen chant circle game – the class play a circle game in preparation for the next activity in which they will plan a development section for the hen chant. The game puts Haydn's musical ideas into a new unplanned order, and also explores the effect of unplanned changes in dynamics, pitch, texture and timbre; all are ways of developing musical ideas.

Hen chant development – in six groups again, the children plan the development of the hen chant musical ideas.

Hen chant sonata form – finally the class perform the hen chant in full sonata form: exposition, development, recapitulation and coda.

Listen to Haydn's musical ideas – relating the chant words to Haydn's musical ideas.

Listen to Haydn's sonata form – identifying the start of each section of Haydn's sonata form.

Listen to The 'hen' symphony, first movement – recognising Haydn's musical ideas and his organisation of them into sonata form.

Hen instrumental in sonata form – creating an instrumental version of the hen chant in sonata form.

What you will need

• CD2 and whiteboard numbering begin again from 1.

Hen chant exposition

1. Teach the class this chant which is made up of six separate, musical ideas (track 1, WB1):

 Joseph Haydn

 And a hen and a hen and a hen, *(repeat these two lines)*

 What a hen,

 What a chicken, *(repeat these two lines)*

 And that Joseph Haydn, how he makes her cluck!

 Chicka chicka chicka chicka
Chicka chicka chicka chicka chick.

2. Divide into six groups – one per idea – and perform the chant with each group saying their musical idea in turn.

What you will need

Teaching tip

At each stage, consider the effectiveness of these unplanned changes. Which effects do the children feel work well? Which would they like to adopt in a planned development?

What you will need

Teaching tips

What do the children think of the development? Does the order feel right? Is it too long/too short? Is the texture too simple, too complex? Are changes in dynamics, timbre and pitch clear? Is the performance neat or untidy – do they need a conductor? (One child might tap a steady beat to keep the chant rhythmical.)

Hen chant circle game

1. Each child secretly chooses either the first or second musical idea. They say their words out loud in turn round the circle, giving the ideas a new order, eg:

2. Repeat, but this time, each child secretly decides whether to say their words loudly or quietly.

3. Now each decides on a way to vary their vocal timbre and pitch, eg saying the words in a scratchy hen-like, high-pitched voice. In another round of the game, you might vary the texture by appointing a conductor to bring the children in one, two, three or more at a time.

Hen chant development

1. Divide into six groups again and practise saying the chant in the original order (the exposition) – each group saying their idea in turn.

2. Explain that you are going to develop the ideas, using methods you explored in the circle game.

   Developing the first subject: ask the two Joseph Haydn and hen groups to decide on an effective development of their two musical ideas (WB3). They should decide on order, dynamics, timbre, pitch and texture and find a way to write all this down so that they can remember it.

   Developing the second subject: in the same way, the remaining four groups develop their four musical ideas (WB4).

3. Now all six groups develop all the musical ideas from both subjects.

4. **Completing the development**: finally, order the sections into a complete development. Make a large plan for everyone to perform from, eg

1st subject	2nd subject	1st subject	Both	2nd subject

Hen chant in sonata form

I. The class, in six groups, now performs the chant in sonata form:

Exposition – perform the chant, each group saying one of the ideas.

Development – perform the complete development devised by the groups.

Recapitulation – repeat the exposition.

Coda – choose an ending, eg all together say very loudly 'What a hen!'

What you will need

WB 5

Listen to Haydn's musical ideas

As they listen to tracks 2-4 (WB6), the children will be able to hear the relationship between the chant words and the six musical ideas which Haydn uses to create the first and second subjects of his exposition.

What you will need

2-4))) WB 6

Listen to Haydn's sonata form

Track 5 (WB7) identifies the beginning of each section of the sonata form Haydn uses: exposition, development, recapitulation, coda. Notice and identify the six musical ideas each time they appear.

What you will need

5))) WB 7

Listen to Haydn's 'hen' symphony

Use WB8 to check that the children are identifying all the main events in *The 'hen' symphony*, first movement:

What you will need

6))) WB 8

Exposition

First subject – the two ideas, 'Joseph Haydn' and 'and a hen', are played several times by violins and flutes.

Link (ending with a falling run of short, crisp notes played on violins) leads to –

Second subject – the violins play the bouncy 'what a hen what a chicken' ideas, then the oboes cluck 'chicka chicka chick'.

Development

The first subject is immediately followed by the second subject, then it is combined with the flutes clucking 'chicka chicka chick'.

The 'Joseph Haydn' idea of the first subject is played forcefully by different combinations of strings and woodwind. The idea is repeated many times at different pitches and combined with energetic running patterns.

Recapitulation

First subject – reappears briefly.

Link – the falling run leads again to –

Second subject in the major key with flutes clucking 'chicka chicka chick'. The music pauses on a long, held note, then –

Coda

The violins play the clucking idea for the last time.

Hen instrumental in sonata form

What you will need

• Copies of WB9 for each of the six groups/individuals.

• A range of instruments from which to choose six – one for each musical idea, eg

1. Begin by deciding whether to work together as a class of six groups, or in independent groups of six players each.

2. Explain that as a class/independent group, the children will build up a piece in sonata form, in which they transfer the rhythms of the hen chant onto percussion instruments of their choice.

3. Whether as a class or in groups, the children need to experiment and discuss how many times to play the first and second subject ideas, how to develop the ideas, recapitulate them and bring their piece to an end. They use the chart on WB9 to show the order:

4. When they are ready, they perform their composition. Together, consider whether:

— the structure of the piece is clear (can each section of the sonata form be identified by the listeners now that there are no words to help?);

— they have made good use of the instruments (eg playing loudly and quietly, using different techniques to produce a range of timbres, contrasting them, combining them, etc).

Classical A Christmas carol

WHAT YOU NEED TO KNOW ABOUT A CHRISTMAS CAROL

Composer: Caleb Ashworth

★ In 1762, Caleb Ashworth published 'A collection of tunes' which were 'designed for those who have made some Proficiency in the Art of Singing'. Only about one in ten country churches had an organ by 1800, so at this time rural choirs sang unaccompanied or with small bands of instrumentalists.

This Non-conformist Christmas carol for voices in three parts and would have been sung in English country parish churches.

Features of the music

★ This carol is for soprano (high), tenor (middle) and bass (low) voices. Like many Non-conformist hymns the melody is sandwiched between a descant (high part) and a bass (low) part. In some verses both the descant and the melody are sung by soprano and tenor voices at their own pitch.

★ Each verse has a different musical texture. A bassoon plays along with the bass voice in all verses.

ABOUT THE ACTIVITIES

Singing A Christmas carol – learn to sing the carol melody then accompany it with a simplified version of the bass line.

Listen to A Christmas carol – focus on the texture of the parts: the arrangement of the carol melody for the different voices.

Perform A Christmas carol – consider texture in arranging a final performance.

	Verse 1	Verse 2	Verse 3	Verse 4
Descant	soprano/tenor		tenor	soprano/tenor
Melody	soprano/tenor	soprano	soprano	soprano/tenor
Bass	bass and bassoon	bass and bassoon	bass and bassoon	bass and bassoon

What you will need

 7-8 WB10-11

- Copies of the songsheet and bass line for all singers and instrumentalists.
- Low-pitched tuned instruments, eg bass xylophone, keyboard, with notes: D G A B D'.

Teaching tip
Teaching the song: all listen to it several times, then join in singing the first two lines of each verse, then all four. Finally sing all four verses.

Sing A Christmas carol

1. Teach the song to the whole class using track 7 (WB10).

> Let an anthem of praise and a carol of joy
> Each tongue and each heart in sweet concert employ:
> This day sprung at Beth'lem a plant of renown
> And Christ to redeem us abandoned a crown.
>
> Conceived of a virgin! How humble his birth,
> Not graced with the pomp and the grandeur of earth
> But laid in a manger, with beasts, at an inn;
> No room for the Saviour of Israel within!
>
> The shepherds with pleasure saluted the morn
> When Jesus, the Shepherd of Judah, was born;
> The sages with wonder acknowledged his star
> And brought him their homage and gifts from afar.
>
> Great Saviour, the tribute of honour we pay
> And celebrate gladly this festival day:
> We triumph in Britain thy glory to see;
> Not sages nor shepherds more happy than we.

2. Choose a small group to work out and play the bass line, track 8 (WB11). When they are confident, ask them to play it to the class.

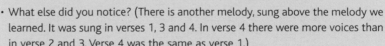

Listen to A Christmas carol

What you will need

 9  WB 12

Listen to the verses one by one, and ask the children to focus on: the melody in verse 1; the bass line in verse 2; any extra part(s) in verse 3; what happens in verse 4.

Questions you might ask

- Did you recognise any of the parts? (The melody was the same as the one we sang. Our bass line was similar but their basses sang extra notes.)

- What else did you notice? (There is another melody, sung above the melody we learned. It was sung in verses 1, 3 and 4. In verse 4 there were more voices than in verse 2 and 3. Verse 4 was the same as verse 1.)

Perform A Christmas carol

What you will need

WB10-11

1. Now perform the melody with the bass line.
2. Ask the children for ways to vary the textures of each verse, eg
   1 solo voice and bass; 2 three voices with bass;
   3 all voices, no bass; 4 all voices with bass.

Are the singers and instrumentalists combining well? Does the volume of the accompaniment complement the different textures chosen for each verse?

Classical Ein Mädchen oder Weibchen

WHAT YOU NEED TO KNOW ABOUT EIN MÄDCHEN ODER WEIBCHEN

Composer: Wolfgang Amadeus Mozart (1756–91)

★ This aria (song) comes from Mozart's comic opera, *The Magic Flute*, which he composed in the last year of his life. The owner of a popular theatre near Vienna commissioned the music and wrote the German libretto (opera script). Despite his failing health, Mozart conducted from the fortepiano (early piano) at the first performance in September 1791. It immediately became one of his most popular operas.

Features of the music

★ The comic character, Papageno the birdcatcher, accompanies Tamino on a quest through enchanted lands to release an imprisoned princess with the aid of a magic flute and bells. Papageno, however, is also on a quest of his own and in the aria *Ein Mädchen oder Weibchen* ('a maiden or a wife') describes his search for a wife. The aria is accompanied by the orchestra and features a glockenspiel as the magic bells.

ABOUT THE ACTIVITIES

Sing an aria – learning to sing an English version of *Ein Mädchen oder Weibchen*, Papageno the birdcatcher's song from *The Magic Flute*.

Listen to *Ein Mädchen oder Weibchen* – focussing on the 'magic' sounds Mozart uses in his accompaniment to the aria (sung in the original language).

Magic accompaniment – composing accompaniment music to the aria, including magic spell music to use as interludes between repeats of the aria.

What you will need

🔟))) | WB 13

Sing an aria

1. Teach the children this English version of Papageno's song from *The Magic Flute* using track 10 (WB13):

> O maiden come to join me, be Papageno's wife,
> A turtle dove beside me, that's all I ask of life!
> Each day would be feasting and pleasure,
> I'd envy no monarch his treasure,
> And that's all the wisdom I need,
> My life would be heaven indeed!

Listen to Ein Mädchen oder Weibchen

What you will need

11))) | WB 14

Explain that the children will hear Papageno's song sung in German, Mozart's language. Ask them to notice the magic bell sounds.

Questions you might ask

- At the beginning the magic bells play a melody with the orchestra. What do you notice about this melody? (It is the same as the first melody sung by Papageno.)
- Do you hear the bells play when Papageno sings? (No, but they play short patterns inbetween the lines of his song.)
- When do the bells play on their own and what do they play? (Before Papageno sings a second melody the bells play the first part of it as an introduction.)
- What happens after Papageno sings the second melody? (The whole thing is repeated; there are different words.)

What you will need

🔟))) | WB 15-16

- Finger cymbals, bells, or bell tree.
- Glockenspiel notes C D E F G and a small hard beater.
- A magic flute: use panpipes, recorder, whistles.
- Magic bells: use finger cymbals, jingle bells, glockenspiel.
- Any other magical soundmakers, eg effects on keyboard.

Magic accompaniment

1. Ask individual children to devise a rhythmic accompaniment for the song, using finger cymbals, jingle bells or a bell tree. Try out their ideas while the rest of the class sing the song (WB15).

2. Select an individual to practise a magic bell glissando – fast slide of notes to add to the song (WB15):

   – after 'wife' – slide the beater quickly over bars C D E F G.

   – after 'life' – slide the beater quickly over bars C D E F.

3. Choose a small group to devise magic spell music to play between repeats of the aria (following the directions on WB16). If you are singing along with the track provided, allow a pause for the spell music, then play the track again from the beginning.

4. Select a conductor to bring the different groups in at the appropriate times in a final performance of your aria.

Teaching tip
Check that the instrumentalists are able to play confidently in time without interrupting the flow of the singing.

Classical links

WHAT YOU NEED TO KNOW ABOUT THE MUSIC

The three pieces of music in this section are linked to the three pieces the children have worked on in depth in previous activities. They are examples of

– orchestral music by Haydn;

– a concerto movement in 'pastoral' style;

– chamber music by Beethoven based on Papageno's song from *The Magic Flute*.

Second movement from The 'hen' symphony
Composer: Joseph Haydn (1732–1809)

This extract is the opening of the second movement. Listen for these features:

– a smooth, quiet melody on the strings;
– a falling phrase on woodwind leading to a repeat;
– two loud, fast falling runs of notes;
– a regular 'clucking' getting quieter and quieter;
– a sudden loud burst of sound by the whole orchestra.

Pastorale
Composer: Pieter Hellendaal (1721–99)

Hellendaal was a Dutch composer, violinist and organist, who studied in Italy then lived and worked in England.

Pastorale is from his violin concerto (1758). It depicts the scene around the crib in Bethlehem as the shepherds play bagpipes to the baby Jesus. 'Pastorale' was the term for a popular type of music of the period in which an idealised vision of the countryside was portrayed in gentle, lilting rhythms, often with drones (page 6) imitating the sound of bagpipes. Hellendaal's orchestra consists of strings, woodwind and harpsichord.

Variations on Ein Mädchen oder Weibchen
Composer: Ludwig van Beethoven (1770–1827)

In 1797, six years after the first performance of *The Magic Flute*, Beethoven composed twelve variations for cello and piano on *Ein Mädchen oder Weibchen*. You will hear

– Theme – on piano with cello accompaniment;
– Variation 2 – theme on cello with piano accompaniment;
– Variation 4 – parts of theme on cello, piano answers.

ASSESSMENT GUIDANCE

★ Can the children develop ideas within a musical structure (sonata form)?

★ Can they suggest improvements to their own and others' work?

★ Can they identify features in music and use correct musical vocabulary to describe the use of musical elements?

★ Can they use simple notation to perform a tuned accompaniment with a song?

★ Can they select sounds and compose using a variety of textures, showing an awareness of how the parts fit together?

★ Can they listen to music, hearing and describing the different sounds using a wide range of musical vocabulary?

ABOUT THE ACTIVITIES

This section enables the children to work independently with three pieces of music which have links to things they have heard and learned during the earlier activities.

What you will need
12))) | WB 17

What you will need
13))) | WB 18

What you will need
14))) | WB 19

Beethoven

Romantic introduction

WHAT YOU NEED TO KNOW ABOUT THE ROMANTIC PERIOD

★ At the end of the 18th century, writers, painters and philosophers began to explore new ways of expressing human emotion. These new 'romantic' ideals were soon adopted by composers, who began to make their music describe feelings and moods, pictures and stories, mystery and adventure. They freed themselves from the formal structures of the classical period and allowed the content or ideas of the composition to determine the structure.

★ They used more colourful, and often larger combinations of instruments. The range of the orchestra was extended by adding lower-pitched instruments such as bass clarinet and tuba, and higher-pitched instruments such as piccolo.

★ Public concerts and musical evenings, soirées, in the home became a regular feature of social life for the middle classes. The patronage of the very wealthy, which had sustained composers and musicians in earlier times became less significant. The demand for large- and small-scale music came from a much more public audience. Music-making in the home consisted of songs, piano pieces, and chamber music (music for a small group). Composers wrote pieces for a wide variety of instrumental combinations, often according to the requirements of particular players.

★ The piano became a very important solo instrument in the 19th century, and an enormous quantity of music was composed for it in the romantic style. Several technical developments to its construction were made, which gave the piano a wider range of notes, volume and tone.

★ With industrialisation and an increase in affluence, many moderately wealthy families bought pianos and enjoyed music-making in the home. While the virtuoso composer/performer was the star of the concert hall and salon, a huge repertoire of music was also becoming available to the amateur player.

★ Exhilarating new dances appeared in the 19th century ballrooms of Europe. Both the waltz and polka were partner dances which developed from regional folk dances and became so popular that they were used by composers for concert music as well as in the ballroom.

Romantic The 'trout' quintet

WHAT YOU NEED TO KNOW ABOUT THE 'TROUT' QUINTET

Composer: Franz Schubert (1797–1828)

★ Franz Schubert was born in Vienna, a great musical centre in his day. He was taught the violin by his schoolmaster father, a keen amateur musician, and the piano by his elder brother. In 1808 he became a choirboy and began a formal musical education.

★ He composed 600 songs in his short lifetime, writing the first as a teenager. In 1819, two years after composing a song called **The trout**, he reused the song's melody in a quintet (piece for five musicians).

★ The quintet was commissioned by a wealthy mine owner and amateur cellist, Sylvester Paumgartner who wanted a piece of music for piano, violin, viola, cello and double bass, which were the instruments which he and his friends could play.

★ **The 'trout' quintet** has five movements (separate sections) and is recognised as one of Schubert's finest works. The fourth movement is a set of variations based on the melody of **The trout**. The theme (melody) and four of the six variations (1, 2, 3 and 5) are explored here.

Features of the music

★ The instruments used are: violin, viola, cello, double bass and piano (WB1).

ABOUT THE ACTIVITIES

Reading a score – the children notice some of the features of the graphic score, which has been specially created to represent Schubert's music. They notice the instruments which he uses and the fish symbol which represents the theme.

Listen to the theme – they focus their listening on the theme and which instruments play it, familiarising themselves with the sounds of the instruments.

Listen to the accompaniment – they focus this time on the way the accompaniment parts in each variation have been notated in the score.

Listen to and notate the missing parts – as they listen to each accompaniment part which is missing from the score, each child devises a way of notating the missing parts.

violin

viola

cello

double bass

piano

Reading a score

1. Explain that the children are going to hear a set of variations by Schubert based on a theme from his song called *The trout*. Use WB1 to familiarise the children with the sounds of the instruments he uses.

2. Together look at WB2, noticing the fish motif which indicates the theme.

3. Now look at the graphic score, WB3-7, noting which instrument plays the theme each time. Explain that some parts of the graphic score are missing and they will devise graphics for them later.

Listen to the theme

As they listen to tracks 15-19 (more than once if necessary), the children follow the score, WB3-7, focussing on the theme.

Questions you might ask

• Which instrument plays the theme first (track 15)? (The violin.)

• In Variation 1 (track 16) the theme is played on the piano. What is different? (It sounds higher than when played on the violin; wiggly decorations, trills, are added.)

• What happens to the theme in Variation 2 (track 17)? (It is played by a group of instruments – viola, cello and bass – and the piano echoes parts of it.)

• How does the theme change in Variation 3 (track 18)? (It is louder, more jerky and lower in pitch. It is played by cello and bass.)

• Compare Variations 3 and 5 (track 19). What is similar and what is different? (The theme is low-sounding in both, but the moods are different. Variation 3 is lively and energetic; Variation 5 is smooth and sad.)

Listen to the accompaniment

1. Listen to the music and look at the score, noticing the accompaniment parts which have been notated.

2. Discuss the way the accompaniment sounds have been notated, eg can the children hear the short, jumping bass notes in Variation 1 and see how these have been notated with jumping dots?

Listen to and notate the missing parts

1. Listen to the music, focussing on the instruments which are playing accompaniment parts missing from the score.

2. Each child devises notations for the missing parts and draws them onto copies of the score. When complete, discuss the scores in small groups, comparing similarities and differences.

3. Listen again. How appropriately do the children's notations represent the sounds? Compare with the suggestions provided in WB8.

Romantic Polka

WHAT YOU NEED TO KNOW ABOUT BORODIN'S POLKA

Composer: Alexander Borodin (1833–87)

★ Borodin learned to play the flute and cello as a child and composed his first polka at the age of eight. However, his other lifelong passion was for chemistry. Instead of becoming a full-time composer he trained in science and medicine and, as an adult, managed to compose music while following his main career. Much of his piano music was promoted throughout Western Europe by the virtuoso performer-composer, Franz Liszt, who travelled extensively giving concerts.

Features of the music

★ This takes a well-known musical exercise for children as a starting point for a piano piece in the style of a lively dance, the polka.

★ *Polka* is a piano duet (for two players). Borodin wrote it for himself and for his adopted daughter, Liza. Liza played the simple ostinato (repeated pattern) on which the whole piece is based.

★ This ostinato, often called 'Chopsticks', was a well-known piano exercise for children. The player uses one hand to play a pattern of notes which stretches the hand out from playing next-door notes to an octave (eight notes apart). Children commonly play it with the index fingers of both hands hence the name 'chopsticks'. Borodin added a lively set of simple melodies for the second player.

★ The piece became so popular that other Russian composers, including Nikolay Rimsky-Korsakov, used the same idea in a collection of pieces for piano, and Franz Liszt composed a short prelude to play before it.

ABOUT THE ACTIVITIES

Listen to the *Polka* – focus the children's listening on the ostinato.

Play the *Polka* ostinato – individually, the children learn to play the Polka ostinato.

Listen to the *Polka* melodies – focus on the other melodies being played.

Compose a Polka duet – pairs of children use the ostinato as the basis for making up a new duet, featuring newly composed melodies, and expressive changes in dynamics and tempo. The pairs refine their work for performance.

Listen to the Polka

Focus the children's listening on the 'Chopsticks' ostinato.

Questions you might ask

- What stays the same in this music? (A repeating pattern – ostinato – which is played many times all the way through.)
- What changes do you notice? (At the beginning the ostinato is played once slowly and quietly as an introduction, then it is repeated many times in a fast and lively way, while other melodies are played. At the end the ostinato is played twice, getting quieter and slower.)

Play the Polka ostinato

1. Let the children work out how to play the polka ostinato using copies of WB10. Use keyboards or tuned percussion, or any other melody instrument available with the notes required.

Keyboard players:

F	G	F	G	E	A	E	A	D	B	D	B	C	C'	C	C'
1	2	1	2	1	3	1	3	1	4	1	4	1	5	1	5

Tuned percussion players:

F	G	F	G	E	A	E	A	D	B	D	B	C	C'	C	C'
L	R	L	R	L	R	L	R	L	R	L	R	L	R	L	R

2. When they have had time to practise the ostinato, check that the players are achieving an even, steady beat. Are they able to play the ostinato over and over without a break between repeats? Have they the control to play quietly or loudly, quickly or slowly?

Romantic Polka

Listen to the Polka melodies

Focus the children's listening on the other melodies in **Polka**. Can the children sing any of them?

What you will need

🔘 20))) 🔘 WB 11

Questions you might ask

- How long is each melody? (The same length as the ostinato pattern.)
- Do any of them repeat? (Yes.)
- Do they move at the same speed as the ostinato. (No, they have different, slower rhythms – one melody note for every two ostinato notes.)

Compose a Polka duet

1. In pairs, ask the children to make up a new duet using any of the notes suggested. They may like to try out Borodin's ideas first – these are shown on WB12 along with the ostinato to play along with (track 22).

2. When they are ready to try their ideas, one child plays the ostinato while the other adds the new, made-up melodies. They should then swap.

3. To prepare for a performance in front of the other children, each pair needs to:
   - decide who will play the ostinato and who will add the melodies (or perhaps they will take turns);
   - decide on the order in which to add the new melodies;
   - consider how tempo and dynamics might be used to change the character of the music;
   - decide on how to coordinate tempo and dynamic changes;
   - practise enough to play confidently to the class.

What you will need

🔘 22))) 🔘 WB 12

- keyboards or xylophones with these notes:

Teaching tips

Discuss what might help the pairs coordinate tempo and dynamics, eg writing a plan of the music showing where changes take place; watching each other and giving pre-arranged signals; listening carefully to each other and responding to changes in each other's playing.

Assess whether the children have been able to make up new melodies which work well with the ostinato. Have they considered tempo and dynamics? Are they able to carry out their intentions successfully in performance?

Romantic Waltz from Serenade for strings

ABOUT THE ACTIVITIES

Listen to this – responding to the music by thinking of the scenes or pictures it conjures up.

Listen to *Waltz* – listening again in the knowledge that the music was intended to create an image of a ballroom filled with waltzing couples.

Compose a musical picture – using instruments of one family, groups choose a picture to describe in music, by creating a matching musical mood.

WHAT YOU NEED TO KNOW ABOUT WALTZ FROM SERENADE FOR STRINGS

Composer: Peter Tchaikovsky (1840–93)

★ Tchaikovsky showed a keen interest in music as a child, and began piano lessons when he was four. Despite his ability in music he became a lawyer, but abandoned this career to become the successful composer of well-known works such as *The Nutcracker* ballet and the *1812 Overture*.

★ The *Serenade for strings* was first performed in 1881 and has four movements (separate sections), the second of which is a waltz. It was a work of which Tchaikovsky was particularly fond. He used an orchestra consisting only of strings (violins, violas, cellos and basses); 'the more strings the better', he said. This gives a rich, smooth, romantic quality to the music.

Features of the music

★ The whole serenade is built on the use of scales (a sequence of adjacent notes). The graceful waltz melody opens with a rising scale:

I	2	3	I	2	3	I	2	3	I	2	3
	B♭	C	D	E	F	G		A	B	D	

★ This is accompanied on the lower strings by the 'um cha cha' rhythm typical of waltzes, but this remains in the background as the strong melody conjures up a picture of 19th century ballrooms and swirling couples.

Romantic Waltz from Serenade for Strings

Listen to this

Questions you might ask

- Without telling the children the title of the music, ask them if the music makes them think of a scene or picture as they listen? (Point out that music makes people respond in different ways, sometimes in thoughts of pictures or stories, sometimes creating a feeling or mood. Their interpretation may be quite different from the composer's intentions.)

What you will need

23))) | WB 13

Listen to Waltz

Reveal the title, show the waltz picture on WB14 and listen again. Does the music create an image of a ballroom filled with dancing couples?

What you will need

23))) | WB 14

Compose a musical picture

1. Divide into groups and ask each group to choose a picture, explaining that they are going to create a piece of music to match the scene. The groups need to talk about the mood they want to give to their music, eg will it be exciting, frightening, joyful, energetic, tiring?

2. Next the groups choose a family of instruments which they think can describe this mood. Try out some ideas with the instruments.

3. To organise their music, the groups might consider these questions:

   – can you use your picture as a score, showing you when to play or will it simply give you ideas?
   – will you need a conductor?
   – will your music have a beat or will the sounds be played freely?
   – when will it be loud or quiet, fast or slow, smooth or spiky, high or low?

4. Give the groups opportunities to record and listen back to their music as they work. Ask them to refine their ideas, considering, eg whether they can make it describe the mood of their picture more clearly; whether they can hear all the sounds or if it is sometimes too crowded, etc.

5. When they are ready, let each group perform their piece to the class.

   The listening children need to consider what they think of or feel as they listen to each group's composition. (This may not correspond with the chosen picture, but there may be valid reasons for the children's feelings. What made them feel this way? Eg 'the tinkly sounds made me feel cold'.)

What you will need

 WB 15-18

- Each group's chosen WB picture.
- Sound recording equipment.
- Instruments divided by the children into families, eg

String – guitars, violins, autoharps, home-made zithers (elastic stretched over open box)

Wind – recorder, whistles, panpipes, flutes, plastic tubes, bottles

Untuned – claves, castanets, wood blocks, cymbals, guiro, bells, triangles, tambours

Tuned – chime bars, gato drum, xylophone, glockenspiel, metallophone

Romantic links

WHAT YOU NEED TO KNOW ABOUT THE MUSIC

The three pieces of music in this section are linked to the three pieces the children have worked in depth on in previous activities. They are further examples of

— chamber music;

— solo piano music;

— music for a grand state occasion.

Scherzo from The 'trout' quintet
Composer: Franz Schubert (1797–1828)

This movement is the third of five: its title means 'playful'. Its tempo is indicated *presto* – very fast. The strongly rhythmical melody is introduced by all the instruments, then fragments are passed back and forth from strings to piano. The joyful mood is emphasised by the speed and the energetic rhythms.

Le rossignol
Composer: Franz Liszt (1811–86)

Liszt was a Hungarian pianist whose virtuoso playing led to the popularity of piano recitals across Western Europe in the 19th century. He was also a renowned composer and piano teacher, often composing pieces of great technical difficulty, which were innovative in exploring the sounds and textures of the piano. *Le rossignol* (nightingale) opens with rising patterns then repeated notes at the top of the piano's range to imitate the song of the nightingale of the title. A long trill (adjacent notes alternated very quickly) and cascading, harp-like sounds lead into a slow, expressive, romantic melody. (Answer to 3: acacacacdb.)

Sursum corda
Composer: Edward Elgar (1857–1934)

Sursum corda was composed in 1894 for a visit to Worcester Cathedral by the future King George V. Its Latin title means 'lift up your hearts' and the music is for strings, brass, timpani and organ. Listen for
– a downward leap by the brass;
– a swelling crescendo accompanied by timpani roll;
– a slowly rising, expressive melody on the strings;
– the brass returning with the solemn opening;
– the development of the string melody.

ASSESSMENT GUIDANCE

★ Can the children use a graphic score to follow music as they listen?

★ Can they use graphic notation to record what they hear in a piece of music?

★ Can they maintain regular repeating melodic patterns (melodic ostinati)?

★ Can they compose and perform regular repeating melodic patterns over a given ostinato?

★ Can they work and perform as part of a group without adult intervention?

★ Can they compose music which communicates different moods and effects, in response to a visual stimulus?

★ Can they describe how music is used to communicate different moods and effects using a wide range of musical vocabulary?

ABOUT THE ACTIVITIES

This section enables the children to work independently with three pieces of music which have links to things they have heard and learned during the earlier activities.

20th century introduction

WHAT YOU NEED TO KNOW ABOUT THE 20TH CENTURY PERIOD

★ The 20th century saw an explosion of different explorations in music, with many varied styles and influences emerging from the late 1800s onwards.

★ At the turn of the century, French Impressionists were experimenting with new ways of painting the effects of changing light, movement and colour in nature. French composers used changing timbres and chords to give musical impressions of similar subjects – clouds, rain, snow, sea.

★ Impressionist composers organised sounds in a new way. They used subtly changing harmonies, free rhythms often sounding like improvisations, descriptive instrumental timbres and textures – almost as though they themselves were painters, using sounds like brush strokes.

★ American composers developed their own distinctive music during the century, often influenced by popular American culture, especially blues and jazz. Aaron Copland was keen to provide audiences with an 'American style' and many of his compositions contain entertaining references to American life.

★ By the end of the century composers were writing music for many different uses: for concerts; theme and background music for TV and film; music for dance, theatre and opera; pieces for special players or groups of musicians; and music for anniversaries, celebrations and state occasions.

★ Twentieth century composers had an increasingly vast wealth of easily accessible music and instruments from other cultures to draw on for inspiration. Many composers began fusing different styles and influences in their compositions to create exciting new sounds.

20th century Gnossienne no 3

WHAT YOU NEED TO KNOW ABOUT GNOSSIENNE NO 3

Composer: Erik Satie (1866–1925)

★ Satie began his musical education with a local organist who introduced him to medieval plainsong. At the age of thirteen he began to study music at the Paris Conservatoire but his teachers were not impressed with his skills. His compositions were often thought to be eccentric. They are littered with obscure instructions to the player: 'arm yourself with clairvoyance'; 'open the head' appear on this piece.

★ His two sets of piano pieces, *Trois gymnopedies* and *Trois gnossiennes* (1890), seem to be dances inspired by ancient worlds: Greece and Knossos. This version of *Gnossienne no 3* has been arranged for orchestra by Ronald Corp. Satie's use of unusual scales gives the piece an unfamiliar and intriguing quality. His unconventional approach to composition was characteristic of the experimental mood amongst many composers at the beginning of the century.

Features of the music

★ Simple step-by-step melodies are played by harp, flute, oboe and violin in turn, while the body of the orchestra plays an accompaniment pattern.

★ The melodies are based on three sets of notes (scales) which are unusual.

★ These melodies move in two contrasting ways:
1. each note is played then immediately repeated;
2. notes are played one at a time in rising and falling waves.

★ The accompaniment is a simple repeating rhythm using a limited number of chords based on the three scales.

ABOUT THE ACTIVITIES

Listen to *Gnossienne no 3* – forming impressions of the piece, using movement and graphics as well as words.

Gnossienne scales – becoming familiar with the sound of the scales which Satie uses in the piece, then creating new scales of their own.

Listen to *Gnossienne no 3* – following a score and recognising Satie's scales.

Gnossienne chords – using voices to build and become familiar with Satie's chords.

Chord changing – practising smooth, quick changes of chord in response to a conductor.

Chord sequences – in pairs, composing a short piece made of a sequence of Satie's chords.

Satisfactory – in groups of four or more, using Satie's chords and scales to create a new piece which moves in a similar way to Satie's music.

Listen to Gnossienne no 3

What you will need

27))) WB 1*

*Whiteboard display numberings begin again from 1.

Ask the children for their impressions of the piece. They may like to move, paint or draw as they listen, or describe their reactions in words. Discuss their responses and how these link with the features of the music, eg the repeated notes, the rising and falling waves of notes.

Gnossienne scales

What you will need

28-30))) WB 2-3

• A keyboard, glockenspiel, or xylophone with the notes of scales 1, 2 and 3:

scale 1

scale 2

scale 3

• Several sets of chime bars or other tuned percussion for individual work.

1. Explain that a scale is a set of notes arranged in order from lowest to highest. Satie used the notes of three unusual scales to make up his melodies in **Gnossienne no 3**. To become familiar with them, choose one child to come out and play a short pattern using the notes of scale 1. The rest of the class immediately sings back the pattern to la (WB2, track 28):

Continue with new patterns, eg

2. Repeat with scales 2 and 3 and different players (tracks 29 and 30).

3. Now each child invents their own five or six-note scale and composes a simple melody (WB3). They need to try out different sets of notes until they find one they like. Ask them to write down the notes of their scale then compose a simple melody using these notes.

4. Listen to the melodies and compare the chosen sets of notes. Together, notice the effect their choice of scale has on melody. (Some may result in very familiar-sounding music; others may feel completely unfamiliar.)

Listen to Gnossienne no 3

What you will need

27))) WB 4

Ask the children to follow the plan of the opening of the music (WB4) and indicate with hand signals the repeated note melodies and the wave shape melodies as they listen. Can they recognise when the repeated note melody begins on a new group of scale notes?

Gnossienne chords

1. Explain that a chord is a group of notes played together. Satie chose three chords to use in **Gnossienne no 3**: ACE, DFA and EGB.

2. Allocate the low notes (A,DE) of each chord to one child, the middle notes (CFG) to a second child, and the high notes (EAB) to a third. Number each set of notes, 1, 2 and 3.

Divide the rest of the class into three groups – low, middle and high – and sit each group with their respective player:

low   middle   high

What you will need

31))) WB 5

• Individual chime bars or three xylophones with these notes:

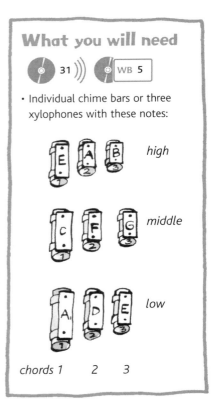

high

middle

low

chords 1   2   3

3. Now use this chord building technique to familiarise the children with the sound of Satie's chords:

Chord 1 – A, C E eg track 31 (WB5)
Low group – the tuned percussion player repeatedly taps the note A, and the others in the group join in by continuously singing or humming the note, breathing as necessary.

Middle group – play, sing and hum the note C continuously, joining in with the low group.

High group – play, sing and hum the note E continuously, joining in with the low and middle groups. All three notes of the chord are now sounding at once.

chord 1   low   middle   high

Chord 2 – D F A, and Chord 3 – E G B
Repeat the process, building the other two chords from low to high in the same way.

When the children are confident at singing the three chords, try building them from the highest to the lowest notes.

What you will need

 32))) WB 6

- Tuned percussion notes as for previous activity.

Teaching tip

Ensure that the children have had enough practice in gradually building the chords one note at a time so they are ready now to change quickly in response to the conductor.

What you will need

 33))) WB 7-8

- Tuned percussion notes as for previous activity.

What you will need

WB 9

Each group will need:

- Melody instruments with the notes for each of the scales (p57), eg

- Tuned instruments for each chord (p58), eg

- Access to sound recording equipment.

Chord changing

1. Work in the same groups as for the previous activity: low, middle and high. Choose a conductor. The conductor will hold up 1, 2 or 3 fingers to indicate which chord to play and sing, eg track 32 (WB6).

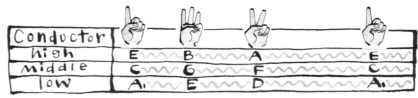

2. Give other children turns to conduct.

Chord sequences

1. Work in pairs. Ask each pair to compose a short piece made of a sequence of chords 1, 2 and 3. They may choose to play all the chord notes at the same time, or find ways of arranging the chord notes in a pattern (eg WB8, track 33):

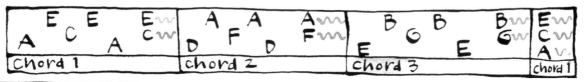

Satisfactory

1. Divide into groups of four or more and explain that each group is going to create a new piece of music based on Satie's chords and scales, which moves in a similar way to Satie's music.

2. Each group chooses one person to play scale 1; the others play chord 1. The chord players decide how to share out the three notes and how to play them, eg overlapping or all at once, repeating the notes or sustaining them.

3. When this is secure, the scale player improvises a melody while the chord players perform their chord.

4. Continue in the same way with the other two scales and chords, changing to a different melody soloist each time.

5. Finally, the groups decide how to put their piece together using all three scales and chords. They play them in different orders and decide which they like (making a sound recording of the work in progress will help). Each group will need to think about how they will signal changes of chord and scale; how many times to play each; how to make a plan of their piece so that it can be repeated.

6. The groups perform their music to the others, who listen carefully and assess both the performance and the music, eg did the players move smoothly from one chord to another, improvise within the given scales, play well together as a group?

20th century Fanfare for the common man

WHAT YOU NEED TO KNOW ABOUT FANFARE FOR THE COMMON MAN

Composer: Aaron Copland (1900–1990)

★ The son of Russian Jews who emigrated to New York, Copland discovered as a child that he was interested in music and by the age of 21 had saved enough money to go to Paris to study composition. After returning to America in 1924 he composed many successful and popular works. He was keen to develop an American style and included jazz rhythms, folk song and square dance melodies in his music.

Features of the music

★ Fanfares are flourishes typically played on trumpets. They have been used for centuries to herald royal or military processions or celebrations. Trumpets were originally valveless and therefore restricted in the notes they could play – the characteristic melodic leaps of a fanfare were determined by this.

★ This is an example of Copland's more serious output. It is played by brass instruments – trumpets and horns – and instruments of the percussion family, which throughout the century received more prominent roles in works of all kinds.

★ The fanfare (1942) was commissioned by the conductor of the Cincinnati Symphony Orchestra as a tribute to the Allied troops involved in World War II. Characteristically, Copland dedicated it to all the 'ordinary people' who win no fame or glory in battle. Unlike most fanfares, it has a slow, solemn mood, but is an impressively moving and optimistic tribute to 'the common man'.

ABOUT THE ACTIVITIES

Listen to *Fanfare for the common man* – following a graphic score of the opening of the fanfare and noticing key features of the music.

Play a fanfare – in pairs, performing a short version of the fanfare.

Compose a fanfare – in the same pairs, composing a new fanfare.

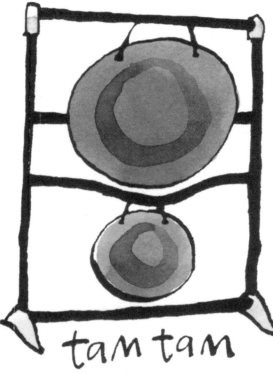

tam tam

What you will need

34-35))) WB 10-11

Listen to Fanfare for the common man

Listen to the sounds of the individual instruments used in the fanfare (track 34, WB10). Next, follow the graphic score on WB11 and listen to the opening of the fanfare (track 35), noticing:

- repetition of three solemn drum beats with tam tam (large gong) on the first of each three;
- trumpets playing leaping phrases in unison;
- repeats of the percussion;
- trumpets' melody returning with horns playing below.

Play a fanfare

What you will need

36))) WB 12

- Pair 1: a drum and a gong.
- Pair 2: instrument with these notes:

player 1

player 2

1. Divide the children into groups of four and again into two pairs. Give them a copy of WB12 and instruments. Pair 1 practises this percussion pattern (note that the first drum beat coincides with the gong):

2. Pair 2 learns to play:

Player 1

G C' G'	C' G' F'	A' F' C' G

Player 2

C G C'	G C' A	C' A F C

3. Finally the pairs join up to put the fanfare together like this (track 36):

G C'G'	C'G'F'	A' F' C G

G C'G'	C'G'F'	A' F' C G
C G C'	G C'A	C' A F C

Compose a new fanfare

What you will need

WB 13

- Percussion as before for pair 1 and for pair 2 any instrument with notes: C D F G C' F' G' A'.

1. The same pairs 1 and 2 compose a new fanfare. They decide whether to make up a solemn or joyful fanfare. They use the percussion and these note combinations in any order:

G	C'	G'	F'	A'	C'

C	G	C'	D	C'	F

2. Together, the pairs decide how many times to play the fanfare and percussion patterns.

20th century Sextet from Dancing with the shadow

WHAT YOU NEED TO KNOW ABOUT SEXTET FROM DANCING WITH THE SHADOW

Composer: Eleanor Alberga (b 1949)

★ Alberga was born in Jamaica and trained in classical music at the Royal Academy of Music in London. She has experience as a member of the 'Jamaican folk singers' and an African dance company. She began composing for the London Contemporary Dance Theatre, has written film scores and a musical setting of Roald Dahl's *Snow-white and the seven dwarfs*.

Features of the music

★ This piece is the final movement from the music for a suite of five dances, **Dancing with the shadow**. It is scored for sextet (six players) playing flute, clarinet, violin, cello, piano and a range of percussion instruments.

★ The first movement of **Dancing with the shadow** is a duet (for two players), the second a trio (for three) and so on to the sextet (for six players). The fast, syncopated rhythms and varied instrumental timbres reflect Alberga's richly diverse musical background.

★ Alberga uses the different timbres of the instruments (eg the congas are played with stick against side as well as by hands on skin).

★ The piece starts with a crescendo (increase in volume) played by two percussion instruments setting a fast, exciting beat. The whole ensemble enters with off-beat rhythms. Short solo sections feature individual instruments as in jazz improvisations. Calmer, slower sections are heard but soon give way to the busy and exhilarating mood of the whole piece.

ABOUT THE ACTIVITIES

Listen to *Sextet from Dancing with the shadow* – identifying the different instruments and changes in mood.

Percussion sextet – working in groups of six to make a composition which contrasts short sounds in a fast tempo with long sounds in a slow tempo.

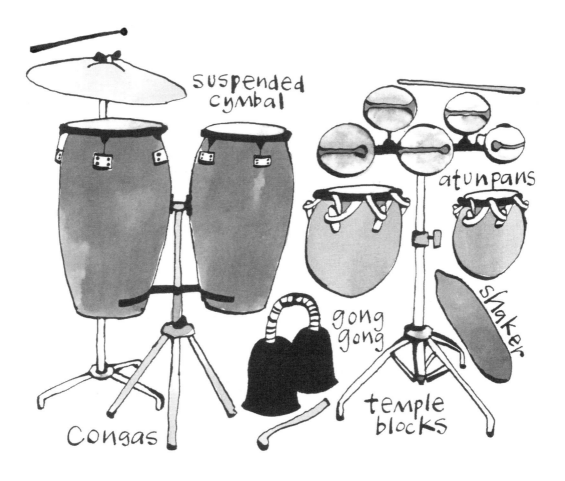

suspended cymbal

atunpans

gong gong

shaker

Congas

temple blocks

Listen to Sextet from Dancing with the shadow

The children will need to listen more than once to answer the questions. Listen all the way through first, then again to answer each question. The timings indicate where to find the answers in the music.

Questions you might ask

- Can you identify the instruments as they are featured? (Piano [35"]; clarinet [47"]; flute and clarinet together [1'05"]; piano and percussion [1'36"]; percussion solo [1'44"].)

- Do you recognise any instruments you have used in school? (Eg shaker, cymbal, woodblock/temple block, etc.)

- Do you notice any changes in the mood during this piece? (It starts in a lively, energetic mood, then there are some calm slower, quieter sections.)

- Can you describe the sound of the clarinet when it first appears? (It plays some very high notes. It sounds smooth as it jumps up and down from high to lower notes [47"].)

- Can you find some smooth, gentle sounds in this piece and describe them? (Flute plays long notes immediately after the clarinet solo [58"]. The violin, clarinet and flute play up and down waves [1'27"]. The flute and clarinet play long, smooth notes [2'].)

Percussion sextet

1. In groups of six, learn to play the fast section, following the score (WB15, track 38). One person counts out the beat for the others to follow. Learn each line separately, repeating it to a slow, steady beat. Next combine two or more lines, repeating them steadily and accurately (WB16).

2. The groups continue practising until they can play with a quick, steady beat, following the conductor, who now conducts the beat silently.

3. When this is secure, the groups make up a new fast section. Each player chooses their own numbers to play on – or between – (use WB17 to record the new score). Practise separately then combine lines in different ways and make a note of them, eg

1st 8 counts	2nd 8 counts	3rd 8 counts	4th 8 counts
Jo and Ayshe	Jo, Ayshe Siva	All	Carlie and Tim

Make up three or four fast sections in this way.

4. Now the groups make up a slow section of music, layering long sounds, one on top of another (track 39). They decide which combinations they like best, and make a note of the order in which to play (WB18).

5. Finally, having made a score, put together the whole piece of music (WB19). Decide

    – how many different fast sections to play;
    – how many slow sections;
    – how to signal the transition to a new section.

20th century links

WHAT YOU NEED TO KNOW ABOUT THE MUSIC

These three examples give the children the opportunity to explore further examples of 20th century music, linked to the previous in-depth activities:

– another example of Satie's music: an atmospheric extract of ballet music describing night;

– an extract from a piece for string quartet and brass instruments;

– a second example of a fanfare to compare with the Copland Fanfare.

ABOUT THE ACTIVITIES

This section enables the children to work independently with three pieces of music which have links to things they have heard and learned during the earlier activities.

La nuit
Composer: Erik Satie (1866–1925)

This piece is from a ballet, *Les aventures de Mercure* (1924), composed during a period when Satie was collaborating with Jean Cocteau and Pablo Picasso. Together with the choreographer Leonide Massine, they produced several ballets which experimented with Cubist ideas. Set and costume designs were by Picasso and this ballet featured three-dimensional poses set to brief pieces of music. The opening sets an atmosphere of night with dark timbres, low pitches and quiet, slow murmurs.

What you will need

40))) WB 20

Konzertmusik for brass and strings
Composer: Paul Hindemith (1895–1963)

This is one of a group of pieces, composed in 1931, which Hindemith wrote for different combinations of instruments. He himself was able to play every orchestral instrument, although his main instrument was viola. For this piece he used a string quartet (two violins, viola and cello), four horns, four trumpets, three trombones and a tuba. The second section, heard here, begins with a strong, rising, three-note melody, contrasted with fast, running melodies on the strings. The instruments take turns to play as if chasing one another.

What you will need

41))) WB 21

Paris fanfare
Composer: Paul Patterson (b 1947)

This fanfare was composed for the state opening of the Channel Tunnel in 1994. It was played on the arrival at Waterloo of Queen Elizabeth II and was broadcast on international television. Patterson combined the opening of the *Marseillaise* with *Rule Britannia* in a triumphant and impressive flourish of brass instruments to symbolise the meeting of the two countries.

What you will need

42))) WB 22

ASSESSMENT GUIDANCE

★ Can the children compose simple melodies using scales as a basis?

★ Can they sing in harmony to create simple chords?

★ Do they understand about the use of pitch, scales and chords to create different moods and effects?

★ Can they compose and perform in parts using scales and chords?

★ Can they compose and perform fanfares in parts?

★ Can they follow a graphic score as they listen to a piece of music?

★ Can they interpret and perform a rhythmic piece using a graphic score?

★ Can they describe, compare and evaluate different kinds of music using appropriate musical vocabulary?